The Story of a Marriage

Rod Broome

The Story of a Marriage

Typeset in Alegreya

Editing, design, typesetting and publishing by UK Book Publishing

www.ukbookpublishing.com

ISBN: 978-1-912183-99-9

This book is dedicated to

ANITA,

My lifetime partner, lover, companion and best friend.

Introduction

What you are about to read - should you choose to do so - is a love story. But this is a real life love story, about real people, and not a flowery piece concerning two fictional characters who are placed in a romantic situation where their eyes meet across a crowded room.

Although, come to think of it...

Perhaps I'd better begin with the cover of this book. The picture is from a card that was given to me by my wife, Anita, many years ago. I cannot actually remember what the occasion was, but it is likely to have been a wedding anniversary - and she made the card herself. Soon after I received it I decided to put it in a little frame and hang it on the wall of my 'office' and it has been there ever since.

When I began to write this book several months after Anita's death it seemed the ideal cover, as it expresses perfectly what we both felt about our fifty-six year relationship - that we were inextricably entwined and supported each other in both easy and difficult times.

After I took it out of the frame to scan it on to the computer I opened it and re-discovered the inscription inside, written in Anita's hand:

My Darling Rod

As we grow older
I'll be constant and true
Just like the ivy.....

All my love always

Anita,

X

The inscription reveals her loving and caring nature with which she was blessed and with which she blessed me.

But perhaps I'd better begin at the beginning...

PART ONE

Young Love

Chapter One

The Beginning

Anita Stanley was born on 15th July 1940 and lived as a child in a little terraced house in Cheetham Hill, a working class district of Manchester. The Second World War had begun about a year before her birth and her father, Leslie, had been conscripted into the Royal Navy, leaving his wife and child to manage as best they could.

Whilst he sailed the Atlantic, protecting convoys of merchant ships as they brought food and supplies into the country, his wife Anne remained at home caring for the new baby.

Life was not easy. Anne's family lived in St. Helens, some thirty miles from Manchester, so she had little support from relatives and spent the war years wondering, and worrying, whether her husband would ever return.

In spite of a difficult childhood, Anita proved to be a clever girl. She attended St. Marks Infant and Junior School and passed the 11+ examination with flying colours, gaining the highest marks in that year in the whole of Manchester.

At Manchester Central High School for Girls Anita also excelled and although probably quite intelligent enough to progress to University, family circumstances dictated that she apply for a place at Didsbury Teachers' Training College.

* * *

I was born on 6th August 1937 and grew up in Littleborough, a village at the foot of the Pennines some fifteen miles from Manchester. It was close to countryside and the moors yet contained several cotton mills. I was christened Roderick Arnold Broome, being named after Doctor Roderick McGill who was present at my birth, but most people now know me as 'Rod'.

I too came from a working class family. My father was a cobbler in the Boot and Shoe Department of the Littleborough Cooperative Society, and I believe my mother was a pickle-packer for a firm called Beswicks before getting married to Dad.

We lived in a stone terraced house and shared a toilet with a neighbour. I went to Littleborough Central School - Infants followed by Juniors - until I passed the 11+ for Grammar School, which was eight miles away in Heywood, a journey on two buses!

I did not enjoy school and was a very average scholar but on leaving I was persuaded to train as a teacher as they were in short supply at that time.

However, before male students could be admitted to Teacher Training College they had to do National Service, so in 1955 I was recruited into the Royal Army Ordnance Corps where I served for two years, attending the School of Ammunition for several months and eventually working as an ammunition examiner.

On being 'demobbed' aged twenty, I began a two year course at Didsbury Teachers' Training College, and after the repressive regime of the army I really enjoyed the relaxed atmosphere of College.

* * *

My first year was very successful, both in terms of my studies and also my social life. Being rather introverted by nature I was surprised at how well I mixed with the other students - both men and women.

At the end of our first year there was a Going Down Dance at which we said goodbye to all the students who had formed our 'second year' and after the nine week summer holiday we returned as the new 'second years' to take their place.

Our term began two days before the new students were due to arrive, so the place felt empty in comparison with when we had left it. Several of our fellow students were delighted to have gained a study-bedroom in college, having spent their first year 'living out' in lodgings, but for those returning to their old rooms as I was, the place seemed to have a different 'feel' about it – there was a sort of hollow emptiness as though something was missing.

The new students arrived on our third day in college, and we watched them clambering out of taxis at the front entrance laden down with luggage or struggling up the drive with their cases having been dropped off at the bus stop. We second years gave them all the help we could whilst weighing them up carefully. Having the maturity of a whole year's experience behind us, we thought the male students looked young and rather green – they had not had to do military service as we had. We second years had been the last intake before the Government decided it was no longer necessary.

To balance the Going Down dance at the end of our first year, there was a Coming Up dance to celebrate the arrival of the new students about a week after the beginning of the new term.

Although I dressed up for the occasion as usual, I was surprised to discover that I was not looking forward to the event. As proceedings began, I found myself standing just inside the doorway of the Social Room alongside a friend, John, passively observing everything that was happening but not particularly wanting to be part of it.

We had been there for but a few moments when a 'Ladies' Invitation Quickstep' was announced and hosts of young women got to their feet determined to take the plunge and get at least one male partner to dance with that evening. In those days of "partner dancing", girls often had to dance together due to the reluctance of men to take to the floor. Much to my surprise, I saw two of the new students making a bee-line for John and myself, and moments later I had accepted the invitation to join the shorter girl on the dance floor. We moved in silence around the room until the record came to an end and then, being the perfect gentleman, I accompanied her back to her seat and sat down beside her. I felt it was up to me to break the ice.

"Hello, my name's Rod."

"I'm Anita."

"How are you settling in?"

"Fine, thank you."

"Where are you from?"

"Manchester."

"Oh, so you've not had far to travel...."

We stumbled through the first few sentences, but as time passed, our conversation became less stilted until eventually we were talking together quite freely. Anita remembered that I had met and welcomed her when she came for her interview in the spring and had shown her to the waiting area outside the Principal's office. She said that it had been good to chat to someone who knew so much about college and how to go about things. It had made her feel so much more at ease.

During the evening I found out that, like me, Anita had a younger sister, and also like me came from a working class family. She had decided to apply to 'live-in' at College, although it would have been relatively easy for her to return home every night. At home, she shared a room with her sister and it would have been difficult to find a quiet place to study. I told her about a transition *I* had made from 'day' to 'live-in' student when I realised the aspects of college life that I would be missing. By the time the Last Waltz was playing we had struck up a friendship and I decided that the Coming Up dance had not been such a bad affair after all!

Over the next few days, I kept an eye open for Anita in the Social Room, but she was rarely there. I questioned one or two of her friends who told me she was in her study-bedroom working, and gradually I came to realise she was a conscientious and industrious student who felt she hadn't the time to spend every evening talking to young men in the Social Room!

However, when the weekend arrived and everyone had more time to relax, I visited the Social Room at regular intervals confident of seeing her there and resuming our conversation. Imagine my surprise – and disappointment – to learn that she had gone home for the weekend after lectures on Friday afternoon and was not due back until late Sunday evening. It surprised me how deflated I felt. Although there were plenty of young women willing to spend time chatting or dancing with me in the Social Room, I had set my heart on getting to know Anita better, and it just wasn't happening!

Sadly for me, this was to be a regular pattern of events. The more energy I put into trying to see Anita, the more elusive she seemed to become. During the week, our 'free periods' or leisure moments never seemed to coincide, and when weekends came round she frequently went home to spend time with her family in Cheetham Hill, north Manchester.

Nevertheless, when we were together we got on very well, and slowly and gradually our relationship developed. On the rare occasions when Anita remained in college over a weekend, we would sit and chat together in the Social Room, or I would take her to a show at one of the Manchester theatres. I came to realise that I had become very fond of Anita and although for some time my deeper feelings were not reciprocated, she soon saw me as a good friend and enjoyed my company.

Chapter Two

Independence

I had decided half way through my second year that I did not want to return home to Littleborough. Two years earlier during national service, I would have given anything to get back, but now I felt that living at home would be too restrictive and I would be cut off from my friends. And of course, I had fallen in love with Anita and had decided that if I could get a school close to college, I would be able to see her in the evenings during her second year. So when the opportunity arose, I went for an interview with Manchester Education Authority and was accepted by them immediately. For similar reasons, a friend of mine, Rod Ashman, decided that he did not want to go back to Crewe, so he too applied to Manchester and was taken on by them as gratefully as I had been!

As we were firm friends, Rod and I thought that it would be a good idea to share the expenses of a flat fairly close to college, reasoning that even after we had left Didsbury we could still be involved in some of the activities there and see people with whom we had formed relationships. Truth to tell, I think we had enjoyed our time at college so much that we were trying to hang onto it, reluctant to move on to reality.

So every evening we began to scan the pages of the Manchester Evening News in the hope of finding a bachelor pad which we could rent at a knock-down price. Unfortunately, it soon became apparent that the mental picture we had of a modern, well-appointed studio flat set in a leafy suburb would be way beyond our means and that we would have to settle for something far more in keeping with our bank balance.

After her rather unresponsive beginning, Anita finally began to fall for my manly charms and soon we were going out together as girlfriend and boyfriend. I was fascinated by the way she walked. Although she was (and remained) only 5 feet 2 inches tall, she had a straight back and an upright bearing which helped her to walk tall. I would find myself watching for her as she moved from place to place around college, admiring her grace and composure. She told me many years later that although she might have appeared to be confident as she moved around, her posture was a cover for deep self-consciousness and insecurity.

I enjoyed taking Anita out and we took advantage of what the city had to offer us. We went to the Palace Theatre or the Opera House to see blockbuster musicals such as "Grab Me a Gondola", "Carousel", or "The Boy Friend" and spent romantic evenings in the cinema watching films such as "Gigi," "South Pacific", or "That Certain Smile". Unfortunately, we had to miss the end of "The Ten Commandments" in order to get Anita back into college for her 11.00 p.m. sign-in!

During the spring term I was in for a big surprise. Each year, the English Department of the College produced a play to which the College Principal, the entire college staff and distinguished guests were invited. It was a highly prestigious production and parts were allocated only after several auditions had taken place. During my second year the chosen play was "The Importance of Being Ernest" by Oscar Wilde, and one evening when we met in the Social Room, Anita told me she had landed the major part of Cecily Cardew. Being unaware that she had a talent for, or even an interest in acting, I was absolutely amazed. Although I was pleased at Anita's success, I was once again in the position of being unable to see her as often as I would have liked – this time because of rehearsals.

In retrospect I see that I must have been quite a jealous young man. I resented the time Anita spent in going home at weekends and her involvement in activities which did not include me. I know that sometimes I sulked or got angry when I could have been pleased and proud of my girlfriend's success and achievement. I hope I mended my ways during the fifty six years of our marriage!

The play was performed on three consecutive evenings, and at every one I sat in the audience admiring Anita's ability. On the final evening however, I was even more nervous than she was, because her parents were travelling across Manchester to attend the performance and I was about to be introduced to them.

After the final curtain, Anita slipped out from her dressing room and joined me in the Social room. I was taken to meet her mother and father who, like her, were both quite small in stature. Her father, a quiet diffident man, remained in the background but her mother – a small plump lady – shook my hand proudly, having just witnessed her daughter's fine performance. Anita's younger sister Pam, aged about twelve at the time, had come along with them too and was smiling happily. She had helped Anita to learn her lines during her weekends at home, and I discovered that she knew her sister's part almost as well as Anita did herself.

I'm not sure of the impression I made on Anita's parents but I know that I was on my best behaviour, trying to say polite and intelligent things! I had fallen in love with their daughter and I desperately wanted them to approve of me.

Rod Ashman and I began to tour the districts of south Manchester on foot or by bus, in the hope of finding a furnished flat in which to live after we left college. We decided that it should be reasonably close to Didsbury and preferably on a main bus route so we could travel easily to our appointed schools.

It became a difficult and rather depressing search. The flats that we liked were far too expensive, yet many of the ones that were within our financial reach were cold, damp and dingy with a poor standard of accommodation. New premises were totally outside our price range, so we focused on large detached houses which had been converted into apartments. These often had a common entrance (the front door) and contained perhaps five separate units – three accessed from the entrance hall, and two more upstairs. Occasionally, there was additional accommodation in the attic space.

Eventually, we came upon a large, red-brick Victorian house on Mauldeth Road in Withington, a couple of miles north of Didsbury, but still south of Manchester city centre. A short path through a dismal garden led to the front door, on each side of which were large bay windows. The door led into a wide entrance hall from which we were able to access the vacant apartment. Looking back on it now, it provided a poor level of accommodation, even for two healthy young men. There was one large room containing two single beds, a small table and a couple of easy chairs. On one wall was a large Victorian fire-place. The adjoining utility room housed a porcelain sink, an elderly cooker, a couple of open shelves and very little else. It was always damp and chilly. The apartment was not centrally heated of course, but after feeding the pre-payment meter it was possible to feel a little warmth for up to a yard away from the one-bar electric fire I brought from home.

However, despite its bleakness, Rod and I decided to take it. With the help of our families we collected together the basics that we would need to move in, and began to adjust to the idea that we were soon to step out on our own into the big wide world.

Chapter Three

My Proposal

Those students who had been signed up by Manchester Education Authority were contacted in July and told which schools they would be joining in September. Rod and I discovered that we had both been allocated schools on the north side of Manchester – so we telephoned our new head teachers to arrange a preliminary visit.

On discovering that our schools were only separated by a mile or so, we arranged to visit them on the same day and made the long bus journey together. My school, Alfred Street Boys' was (as one might expect) on Alfred Street in the district of Harpurhey, whilst Rod's School – 'Lily Lane' – was unsurprisingly on Lily Lane in Moston, the adjoining district.

One unsettling thing for me was that the school's name contained the word "boys", rather than the expected "junior". I felt even more unsettled as, walking along Alfred Street on that particular morning, I saw a huge two-storey, red brick edifice towering ahead of me. It was much bigger than I had expected and did not at all match my image of a junior school!

However, Dan Stewart, the head, could not have been more pleasant or friendly. He was a short, stockily-built man with a ready smile and a sunny disposition. He greeted me warmly and having asked his secretary to bring us some tea, he set about explaining changes and reorganizations that the Local Authority had in the pipeline.

Apparently, in earlier years Alfred Street School had housed four separate units. There was an infant school and a nursery class on the ground floor, and two separate single-sex schools – for children aged 7 to 15 years – on the first floor under two head teachers. No wonder the building was so large!

Now, the older children from both boys' and girls' schools were in the process of being moved to a new, mixed secondary modern school. Alfred Street was to retain its nursery class and infant school on the ground floor, and eventually a merged junior school would occupy the whole first floor under one head teacher. But, for the present, the junior boys and girls were to remain separated until the final class of secondary age pupils had moved out in a year's time.

Mr. Stewart escorted me around the school, and introduced me to each member of staff. He told them that I would be taking Junior Two Boys during my probationary year of teaching, and the following year girls were to be part of it.

As I journeyed back to college that afternoon I felt reasonably happy. I liked the head and the staff had seemed very friendly. I was eager to tell Anita about my new head teacher, the imposing building and everything that had happened during my visit to the school.

With passing time, Anita and I had become closer and closer. By now we spent most of our free time together and everyone knew that we were going out 'in earnest'. I felt relieved that I had decided to find a flat near to college as I could not bear the thought of being separated from her for weeks at a time. She had said that her parents had thought I seemed to be a nice young man, so at least I knew I had one foot in the door! And when I had taken Anita home to meet my mother and father, everything had gone smoothly and they seemed to approve of her.

One evening, as Anita and I sat in the local cinema watching a film starring child actress Hayley Mills, I was overwhelmed by the feeling that I couldn't bear the thought of ever being parted from her. But I was in turmoil. I had not yet earned my first salary. I hadn't even started my first job. How could I even think of buying a house and supporting a wife? Nevertheless, I was certain that I wanted to share the rest of my life with Anita and I believed she felt the same. Suddenly, on impulse, I leaned towards her and whispered in her ear, "Unofficially, and off the record, will you marry me?"

It would have scored top marks in any 'Most Unromantic Proposal Ever Received' list, but Anita was not put off by that. She knew she loved me and without hesitation said "Yes." We spent the remainder of the film snuggled up to each other as we planned for our future. She often teased me about my proposal afterwards of course and I realised that ahead of me lay the somewhat daunting task of approaching Anita's father for his daughter's hand in marriage. However it gave me courage to know that my feelings were fully reciprocated.

It was still customary in 1959 for a young man to ask permission from a girl's father if he wished to marry her – particularly if she was under 21 years of age. As Anita was only 19 at the time, I felt I had to go through the procedure to get the family's blessing.

I had been invited to tea at Anita's home and we had decided that this would be an ideal opportunity for me to speak to her father. Anita had warned him in advance that I wanted to have a 'special word' with him, so after the meal was finished we retired to the front room, leaving the ladies to wash up in the kitchen. Sitting nervously on the edge of the settee, I declared my love for his daughter, laid out my future prospects, and assured him of my intention to treat her well. I think he felt as awkward as I did, and quickly gave his consent. We invited the waiting ladies to join us and they came in carrying a celebratory pot of tea.

From that moment on our marriage was a certainty, but the custom was that first we must become engaged. When we had saved up sufficient money we could begin to make arrangements for the wedding. As we each came from working class families – neither of which had much money to spare – we knew that it would be our task to save hard so that we could marry within the foreseeable future.

At that time, Anita's parents and sister lived in a tiny two-up, two-down terraced house in the Cheetham Hill district of Manchester. There was no hot water, no garden and the toilet was in the back yard. Anita's father had served in the war as a gunner with the Royal Navy, escorting cargo ships carrying food to Britain across the Atlantic. He had been lucky to survive, as two of his ships had been torpedoed and he had been rescued from the sea after some time in the water. This experience had left him shell-shocked, and his hands would shake at times, particularly if he was under stress or feeling nervous. After convalescence and demobilisation he became employed as a labourer. Anita's mother had spent the war years worrying about her young husband whilst trying to bring up their baby and run a home on very little money. Although their situation was by now much better, the strain of those war years had left its mark.

In many ways my parents had been more fortunate. Although we too lived in a two-up, two-down terraced house in Littleborough, my father, as a cobbler, was in a reserved occupation and did not have to join the Forces. My mother did not have the worry of my father being killed in action, but she often had difficulty in making ends meet as my father was on piece work and sometimes earned very little money. He was also enlisted into the Special Police Force in our village so in addition to working an eleven hour day (when there was work to do that is!) he would be out on patrol several nights a week. Eventually, some years after the war, he was promoted and became manager of the Boot and Shoe Department at our local Cooperative Society, and in time our family was able to move to a larger house – with bathroom – in 1957.

Both our sisters were born at the end of the war. Pam was more than seven years younger than Anita and my sister, Maureen, was almost seven years younger than me. They were delighted at the news of our future wedding and eagerly looked forward to becoming bridesmaids.

And so as I came to the end of my college course the future couldn't have looked brighter. I had gained my teacher's qualification, been given a post in a Manchester school run by the most affable of head teachers, fallen in love with a wonderful girl and found accommodation close enough to college to be able to see her – and other friends – almost every night.

I was determined to be a make a success of my job and earn enough money to buy an engagement ring for Anita. I planned to put something in the bank every month towards a deposit on a house and an early wedding. But as often happens in life, things do not always run according to plan and there were one or two hurdles to clear before all my hopes were to be realised.

Chapter Four

Plans

I began working at Alfred Street School in September 1959 and settled down reasonably well. My charges were a class of Junior Two boys – 39 eight-year-olds – with whom I quickly developed a good working relationship and so did not have too much trouble. They sat in pairs at double desks which were ranked in four blocks facing the front of the classroom. The boys' primary duty was to look at the blackboard as I wrote on it and listen to me when I was speaking. In those days most teachers of young children were women. I was the first male teacher that they had come across and some of them were a little apprehensive, so they took great care not to upset me!

What I taught them was largely down to me. Of course, general guidelines were provided, but there was no detailed syllabus for me to follow. Reading, writing and arithmetic were key subjects and these were on the timetable every day, but in general most class teachers tended to adhere to the programmes of work laid out in the rather elderly text books to be found in most classroom cupboards.

My classroom contained two cupboards filled with reading books. The first housed the class's so-called 'library books' which children could borrow and read in any 'spare time' they had in the classroom. The second contained the 'class readers' – various books assembled from a number of schemes and given out to individual pupils by the teacher. These were designed to help children make progress in their reading ability.

The system was somewhat haphazard and in common with many other teachers I allocated books instinctively depending on what I judged to be the ability-level of each child. Sometimes teachers would attempt to grade the books in their cupboards and stick coloured labels on their spines – so that children within a class would progress from green, to red, to purple, to yellow, and so on. But there was no whole-school plan. Each classroom was an autonomous unit.

* * *

Whilst I was settling in at Alfred Street, Anita, now in her second year at college, was having doubts about having chosen to specialise in teaching secondary children. On her third teaching practice she found herself facing classes of students who were only two years younger than she was and who often towered above her. The situation was very demanding.

Her tutor on this practice was one of her education lecturers and he had a friendly word with her. He said that although he could not fault her preparation or delivery of lessons, he could sense that she was not altogether comfortable with the age-group. He said he thought she was "made to be a junior teacher" and would find teaching younger children much more to her liking. She agreed, so with his co-operation certain major changes were made to the course she was taking. Instead of three science subjects, one at higher and two at a lower level, Anita dropped Physics and joined the English Literature group more than half-way through their course. Her tutor also arranged for her final Teaching Practice to take place in a Junior School.

Of course, these changes involved her in a great deal of extra work. She had to "catch up" with the other students by reading set books which they had already read, and consider how to set about teaching the whole range of subjects as opposed to teaching mainly science. Here her conscientious and studious approach stood her in good stead. Within a short time she was up to date with her studies and was fully integrated into her new group.

* * *

As Christmas drew near I had earned two month's salary and decided that I could afford to buy an engagement ring for Anita. So during the early weeks of December we spent Saturday afternoons trudging around central Manchester, gazing into jewellers' windows in the hope of finding a ring which fulfilled two criteria – to be liked by Anita and to be within a price range that I could afford!

After much searching we found a dainty gold band surmounted by three precious stones – a central square emerald flanked by two miniature diamonds. I cannot quite remember how much it cost but I know it was just under £20, which at that time was almost two thirds of my monthly salary. To us however, its value for what it symbolized was beyond price.

We had decided to become engaged on Christmas Eve and we needed to arrange matters so that neither of our families (who had not yet met) would feel excluded.

Nowadays, this would not have presented a problem as by car the journey from Anita's home to mine would have taken well under an hour. But in those days a journey of sixteen miles on three buses seemed a very long way to travel, particularly as it was during the Christmas period when public transport ran a 'Sunday service'. The burning question was "would there would be appropriate 'connections' between the various stages of the journey"?

After pouring over bus timetables, we decided that I would spend Christmas Eve at Anita's home, and that it *was* possible to travel to Littleborough on Christmas Day to spend the rest of the holiday with my parents. Then another problem arose. Although Anita could stay at my parents' home by sharing a double bed with my sister Maureen, there was absolutely no spare accommodation at Anita's home, as her parents occupied the front bedroom and she and Pam shared the back!

However, undaunted, I dug out an old sleeping bag from my scouting days and, after 'plighting our troth' and being 'toasted' on our engagement on Christmas Eve, everyone retired to bed leaving me to settle down in my sleeping bag on a row of settee cushions which were laid out in a line along the floor. Somehow, I not only 'managed to cope' but had a good night's sleep – to be awakened on Christmas Morning by a loving kiss from my brand new fiancée. Together we breakfasted and after exchanging presents with Anita's family, began the long journey to Littleborough where the celebrations were to begin all over again.

Throughout the Christmas season, Anita flashed her ring proudly wherever we went, and I was delighted to be able to speak of her as my fiancée. With pride I introduced her to my grandfather and other relatives and felt she was warmly received by all of them.

Almost immediately, Anita and I began to discuss how soon we would be able to be married and where we would like to live. I already taught in a Manchester school and Anita – who would be living at home after leaving college until we were married – had not yet applied to a Local Education Authority. We knew that any plans for our future together would have to be deferred until Anita too, was finally qualified and had started to earn a salary.

Chapter Five

Shock!

The short days of January 1960 were as cold and wet as usual and the bachelor pad which Rod and I shared was neither warm nor welcoming to come home to.

By the time I left school, with a briefcase full of marking, it was already dark. After two seemingly endless bus journeys, I would let myself into our cold, inhospitable apartment and then decide what to have for tea. When Rod and I returned home simultaneously we would share in the cooking of our meal and then everything would feel lighter and more fun as we talked about our day. But more often than not one of us would be delayed after school and so we would eat separately. We soon discovered that although we shared accommodation we lived almost totally independent lives.

After plugging in our one-bar electric fire, I would, perhaps, unwrap a meat pie that I had collected on my way home from school and warm up a tin of peas to complete my first course. This would be followed by a cake or custard tart, purchased at the same pie-shop and washed down with a mug of tea. My solitary meal finished, I would settle down to mark my class books, before hurrying out to see Anita.

Because we were short of money and were saving up to get married, Anita and I would spend most weekday evenings strolling around the streets of south Manchester, talking together and window-shopping. From time to time we did go to the cinema, but more often than not we braved the cold north wind and the drizzle for the simple reward of being in each other's company. We held hands and paused in front of furniture shops and house agents' windows, discussing plans and sharing our likes, dislikes and preferences. Although the weather was often bad, in the words of the old song, we had "our love to keep us warm" and at the time that was all that mattered to us. After a few sweet hours, I would either see Anita back to college and then return to my flat or, if it was late, I would put her on the bus in Withington and wave her off as it disappeared from sight.

Whatever we decided to do, we always had to plan it in advance. There were no mobile phones of course and it was difficult to get in touch with Anita at college as the students' telephone was usually in use. Sometimes, I would make arrangements to phone Anita in college at a particular time from a nearby telephone box, only to find the box occupied at the prearranged time. Alternatively, finding it empty, I would dial the college number repeatedly to discover that a string of students were using the college phone preventing my call from getting through. It was less stressful if we decided in advance just when and where we were going to meet.

At weekends, Anita and I would often travel to my parents' home in Littleborough, Anita sharing a double bed with my sister Maureen, or we would spend time at Anita's home in Cheetham Hill where I grew to know her family, especially her younger sister Pam, to whom I became a 'big brother'. During Littleborough weekends we would go for country walks along the hilly paths I had wandered as a child, and when in Manchester we would visit the local municipal parks or stroll around department stores planning the furnishing of our future home. We began to speculate on how soon we would be able to marry after Anita had finished college and to discuss how much money we would need to have saved before that date. But during the month of February 1960 our planning was brought to an abrupt halt.

One Friday evening, Rod Ashman had gone home for the weekend, and Anita had come to spend the evening at the flat. We snuggled together in the big armchair in front of the puny electric fire, talking and cuddling alternately. Unfortunately I had been suffering with a cold for a week or more and on that particular evening I was really under the weather. Anita decided that I needed an early night. She went out to the local corner shop and bought some aspirins and bottles of soft drink in case I felt thirsty in the night and, leaving strict instructions that I was to have two aspirins and a hot drink before going straight to bed, she set off back to college earlier than usual. As she closed the flat door she said that she would return early the next morning and felt sure that I would be feeling much better by then.

She could not have been more wrong! During the night I grew worse. I felt as though I was on fire and I tossed and turned in the bed, every bone in my body aching. True to her word, Anita arrived soon after nine the next morning and was distressed to find that, rather than 'feeling better', my condition had deteriorated.

I told Anita my symptoms and she decided I must have 'flu and that my best course of action would be to stay in bed all day and have lots of cold drinks. Anita stayed with me, tidying the flat to pass the time away and supplying cooling drinks which were all that I could take as eating was the last thing on my mind. It was fortunate that Anita was with me, for as the hours passed by I became worse. My temperature soared, my chest began to ache and I became delirious, losing all sense of reality and talking incoherently.

Anita decided that it was time to telephone the doctor and let my parents know that I was ill before they left the Littleborough shop where they worked, as they did not have a telephone at home. To the doctor's credit, although he had never seen me as a patient before, he came within the hour and arranged for me to be admitted to hospital immediately, saying that he thought I had pneumonia. From that point on, my memory of the next few hours is blurred. When the ambulance arrived I was carried out of the flat on a stretcher, wrapped in a red woollen blanket, and transported to Withington General accompanied in the ambulance by an anxious and tearful Anita.

She gave the necessary information to the hospital staff and I was allocated a bed on a ward where I immediately lapsed into a state of semi-consciousness. Anita was left with the difficult task of somehow getting a phone-message to my parents, to tell them that I was in hospital and seriously ill!

Anita also had to ring college to explain that she might not be back until very late that night. It was already evening and she wanted to stay with me as long as she was allowed to do so, and was not sure of the times of buses back to college from the hospital. Of course the only college telephone number that Anita knew by memory was that of the students' telephone. But fortunately the person who picked up the phone when she rang was one of my friends, Brian Riley, who had stayed on at college to do a third year. He promised to take the message to the college deputy principal, Miss Mackenzie, straight away. She could not have been more understanding or helpful.

She asked Brian (who willingly agreed) to go and collect Anita from the hospital and walk the mile or so back to college with her, as the buses would soon stop running for the day. As he did so, Brian told her she was to report to Miss Mackenzie's flat on her return, and there she was greeted by the Deputy Principal who, quite out of character, was in dressing gown and curlers. Miss Mackenzie put on the kettle and made a cup of tea, and the two of them had a late-night heart-to-heart in her sitting room, Anita pouring out her worries and anxiety about my situation.

On the following morning – Sunday – my procession of visitors began. My parents were given a lift to Withington in Uncle Charlie's Austin Seven (he was the only member of the family to own a car) and Anita met them outside the entrance and they all came in together.

As I had been placed on the free list, family visits were allowed at any time. Pneumonia had affected my left lung and, medical science not being as advanced as it is today, my parents were told it would be some weeks before I was fully recovered. Naturally, everyone was very concerned about me, and arrangements were made for family members to visit every day during the following week – a journey of around twenty miles each way on several buses.

On Monday morning Anita telephoned the hospital to find out how I was, but not only was her request for information refused, she was told that she would not be able to visit me as she was not 'next-of-kin' or a relative. She was distraught! Overwhelmed by frustration and distress she telephoned her mother in Cheetham Hill (via the butcher's shop across the road) who immediately caught a string of buses to get to college in support of her daughter. I don't know if it was the look of determination on my future mother-in-law's face, but when three hours later mother and daughter arrived at the hospital together they marched in unchallenged to see me!

Various aunties made the journey from Littleborough by bus and at times there was a queue of people waiting outside the ward to see me, as a strict rule was in force that only two people were allowed at my bedside at any one time. This caused problems for both Anita and me. Because my relatives had travelled so far to visit me it was natural that they should be given most of the visiting time – which of course meant that Anita and I had very little time together – and that was always under the watchful eye of one of my relatives!

My headmaster, Dan Stewart, who lived in Prestwich, also came to see me a couple of times in his Morris Minor, and on one occasion coincided with Auntie Nellie – my favourite Auntie when I was a child. Although she had a heart of gold, Nellie was not a 'retiring violet' and her behaviour was often loud and boisterous. To my great embarrassment, she spoke to Mr. Stewart in a friendly, but in my opinion, an over-familiar way – joking about school-teachers, the cane and events in my childhood. Thankfully, he took it all in good part and even gave her a lift home to Littleborough at the end of the visit, thus adding fifteen miles to his journey.

One thing I learned from my time in hospital was that as a headmaster Mr. Stewart behaved like a true gentleman, showing me care and concern when I needed it most, even though my long absence – in my first year as a teacher – no doubt caused him considerable inconvenience in the management of his school. It was also brought home to me what I already knew – that my parents and extended family were loving and supportive when I most needed their help.

I was discharged from hospital after ten days, but I did not return to the flat in Mauldeth Road. My parents – Mum in particular – put their foot down. They insisted that I return home to Littleborough and live with them. Mum asserted, probably correctly, that I had been neglecting myself and had brought on the illness by living in a cold, damp apartment and "not eating properly". There was no point in arguing as Anita was of the same mind, and so outvoted and defeated, I returned to reclaim the attic bedroom in my parents' home.

Rod Ashman had been to see me in hospital and he now visited me in Littleborough. I don't know whether it was the relief of being back in the bosom of my family but it didn't occur to me at the time that my unexpected departure must have caused him a great deal of difficulty. He had now become the solitary occupant of our bleak apartment in Mauldeth Road and my absence meant a halving of the monthly income to pay the rent. Nevertheless he showed no animosity towards me when I told him that I would not be returning to Withington and I believe he was fortunate in getting a new flat-mate within a short period of time.

There were many advantages to living in a warm house again and enjoying Mum's cooking, but a major disadvantage was that now I could only see Anita at weekends. So despite all the practical difficulties involved, we reverted to the old system of phoning each other every night using synchronised watches and public telephone boxes. Despite our long loving phone conversations, the weekdays seemed to pass very slowly, and I began to look forward to Friday evening from Monday morning onwards!

Chapter Six

Recovery

U nder Mum's ministering care, I slowly regained my health and strength and after six weeks the doctor declared me fit for work. My journey to school was now more complicated. It involved my catching the eight o'clock bus from Littleborough to Rochdale and then transferring to a Manchester bus which passed through the district of Harpurhey, stopping at the end of Alfred Street at about a quarter to nine. The distance was not much further than when I had lived in Mauldeth Road, but I was travelling south instead of north.

At that time, I was the youngest member of staff at Alfred Street and knew that I had much to learn from the older teachers. The deputy head, Archie Hudson was within a year or two of retiring when I took up my appointment. He was one of the 'old school' – strict but kindly – and was respected by all the pupils. He seemed to be on dinner duty almost every day, wandering around the hall supervising the children as they ate.

The meals were cooked in a neighbouring school and brought in every day in containers. They varied in quality and temperature and were not particularly appetising, but Archie would parade around the hall at the end of each course, holding his empty plate aloft so that everyone could see he had eaten every scrap of food! However, it didn't seem to have much effect on the children as there was always a lot of uneaten food scraped into the pig bin – so called because it was collected by lorry each day and taken to be boiled up to become pig-food.

A few months after his retirement in August 1960, Archie Hudson died unexpectedly. Having no family ties to keep him in Manchester he had moved with his wife to a bungalow just north of Morecambe to enjoy a well-earned retirement. Sadly, it was not to be.

Another Alfred Street teacher who had a profound effect on me was Dorothy Wykes. She had been teaching for many years and taught seven-year-old Junior One children in the classroom next to mine.

Dorothy was seriously disabled. She wore heavy iron callipers on both legs and could only walk very slowly with the aid of two sticks. As I mentioned earlier, the junior school was on the first floor of the building, and the staff room was situated at ground level close to the children's entrance. Whilst the rest of us could run up the twenty five stone steps with ease and pop down to the staffroom for a cup of tea at playtime, climbing the stairs was a major undertaking for Dorothy. She would arrive by taxi long before school was due to begin and embark on the arduous journey to the first floor. It took her all of ten minutes. She then had to struggle along the corridor for a further five minutes in order to reach her classroom.

However, once she was seated behind her high teacher's desk, Dorothy became queen of all she surveyed. Without moving from her chair, she organised the children, the books, the equipment (pencils, rulers, crayons, etc.) in such a way that everything ran like clockwork. She had a network of seven-year-old monitors who collected and distributed books, gave out milk straws, sharpened pencils, took the completed class register to the school office and generally kept the classroom shipshape. What is more, she had no discipline problems whatsoever, the children obeying every word she uttered and never misbehaving or becoming difficult. Her method of discipline was based on firm but good-natured gentleness – and for her it worked.

I had been at the school for a few months when, one lunch time, Dorothy took me aside.

"I hope you don't mind my asking this," she began, "but do you ever speak to the dinner ladies?"

I was non-plussed. A team of four middle-aged women would arrive at school at around 11.30 a.m. and put out the dining tables and chairs in the school hall. Later, when the metal trays containing the meal arrived in a van they would put on white overalls and set up at the front, ready to serve. Afterwards, they cleared everything away and left.

I hadn't consciously been ignoring them, but I had to admit to Dorothy that I had not actually spoken to any of them since I had joined the staff.

She smiled.

"I think they would appreciate it if you said good morning, and had a word with them occasionally," she said. "I know you haven't meant to give the wrong impression, but it's easy to appear stand-offish!"

I was mortified! I had had no intention of offending the ladies, but I suddenly realised that they might have seen my behaviour as 'stuck-up' or condescending. I felt dreadful for the rest of the day, and made sure that I put the situation right over the next week or two. That lesson stayed with me during the whole of my teaching career, and from then on I made a conscious effort never to differentiate between the various roles in school. I had learned that everyone deserved respect and friendliness no matter what job they did.

* * *

As the months passed and summer approached, Anita began to think about applying for a teaching post within travelling distance of home. One day, the education lecturer who had advised her to change to a 'junior' course during her second year, met her in the corridor and offered his help.

"I have a personal friend who is the head of a junior school in Salford," he said, "and I've just learned that there'll be a vacancy at his school from next September. I've known this chap for a long time and he's a very experienced teacher. If you decide to apply for the post, I'll put in a good word for you and explain about the changes you made late in your course. I'm sure he'll take you under his wing and give you any extra help you might need."

Anita appreciated the lecturer's kindness and offer of help, but when she told some college friends about it that evening, one of the girls pulled a long face. She had just finished a teaching practice at the school in question, she said, and had not enjoyed the experience in the least. She considered the head to be fussy and patronising and said she *certainly* wouldn't want to work there!

Put off by the girl's remarks, Anita decided not to take up the lecturer's offer and applied for a teaching post in the usual way. She completed an application form for a teaching position in Salford, and was eventually called for interview at the Education Offices. There, as expected, she was instantly accepted by the Authority and placed on their list.

A few weeks later, Anita heard that she had been given a job at Lower Kersal Junior School – a single storey building close to the Castle Irwell Race Course in Salford. It was a short bus ride and a twenty-minute walk from her home in Cheetham Hill.

She went to meet the head and staff during the summer term and found that it was a three-form entry school, containing twelve classes in all. The head teacher was Arthur Gale who, whilst working as a teacher in Salford in the late 1920's, had been a star player at Chester Football Club and in 1930 had scored an amazing 73 goals in 39 League games, resulting in the election of the club to the Football League. During the next ten years the club was never lower than tenth in the Third Division North.

On this first visit Anita found him standoffish and difficult to talk to. She later realised that he was quite deaf and wondered if perhaps he had had difficulty in hearing what she was saying. He had passed her into the care of Mrs. Quinn, a senior teacher who took her around the building and showed her the classroom where she would be based from the following September. She explained to Anita that she would be the class teacher of Form 1B – the middle stream of first year children – and listed a number of her duties, one of which would be to clean out the class-room fish tank! However, Anita was given no schemes of work from which to plan her lessons and even on this first visit she noticed that there were very few books and little equipment in the cupboards. She left the school wondering how she would get on when she began work there in the autumn.

The summer holidays arrived and Anita gained her Teacher's Certificate and said her fond goodbyes to the many friends she had made during her time at Didsbury Training College. I learned that I had passed my probationary year and was now recognised by the Government Department of Education as a fully-fledged member of staff at Alfred Street Boys School. Eagerly we looked forward to being able to spend more time together during our six-week break, planning our wedding and buying our future home which all at once seemed possible.

Chapter Seven

A Home of our Own

Anita began teaching at Lower Kersal Junior School in September 1960, and from the outset things did not go well. On the first morning she arrived early and after 'signing in' at the head's office, made her way to the classroom that Mrs. Quinn had indicated would be hers when they had met before the holiday.

To her surprise, she found Mrs. Quinn already in occupation, sitting behind the teacher's desk looking through some papers. Although certain that this was the room that had been previously allocated to her – the fish tank was a giveaway – Anita was informed quite sharply that this had never been her classroom. Hers was the one next door! When Anita tried to protest, her words were met with blank denials. It was the first indication of many that led her to realise that she couldn't rely on many things that Mrs. Quinn said. Nor did it take long to realise that the teacher had an exceedingly poor opinion of men. When she discovered that Anita was planning to be married during the following year, her comments were generally critical and disapproving, and it was difficult for Anita to know how to respond without appearing rude. However, after a couple of weeks of enduring Mrs. Quinn's unpleasantness a mature teacher took Anita under her wing and explained the personal family problems that were probably at the root of the senior teacher's bitterness. After that the unkind remarks became less hurtful.

After only a short time, Anita discovered that teaching a class of first year juniors with no schemes of work to guide her, and with little equipment other than a set of old, bitten-down pencils, was a difficult task indeed! Even though she was an inexperienced probationary teacher, she did not have a mentor to look to for help and was not given any support from the Head other than being informed of a number of "rules" which he had formulated over the years and which were trotted out to all new members of staff. He seemed to make no attempt to engage her in personal conversation or to make her feel at home in the school, and he didn't ask if he could be of help in any way.

In short, Anita found her new head teacher to be intimidating, unapproachable and lacking in humanity. For instance, after Anita had been working at the school for a couple of months the local Tax Office rang the school with an enquiry about Anita's national insurance card. The head reluctantly brought her out of class to the telephone to answer their questions, but told her later, in no uncertain terms, that personal telephone calls were not allowed, and it must never happen again!

* * *

Fortunately, Anita didn't have time to brood on her work situation, for in the evenings there were happier things on her mind. For several weeks we had been mulling over where we should live after our marriage, and had come to the rather mundane conclusion that the best location for our new home would be somewhere between Cheetham Hill and Littleborough.

The reasons for our choice were these: we wanted to remain in the north of England to keep in touch with our parents; I was happy teaching at Alfred Street School and did not want to apply for another job after only two years; both of us were rather cautious young people who did not possess a spirit of adventure.

During that autumn we continued to phone each other every evening. I would walk to a telephone box outside the central post office in Littleborough. As the church clock struck eight, I would lift the receiver and dial the number of a call box in Cheetham Hill. Usually the receiver was lifted immediately by Anita who answered the call but occasionally I would hear the engaged tone and have to keep trying until the 'intruder' at the other end had vacated the box.

Our conversation followed a similar pattern every night. We began by declaring our undying love for each other and asked about each other's day before exchanging information about the houses that were advertised for sale in our local newspapers. The Manchester Evening News was delivered to Anita's home every evening and the Rochdale Observer came out on Wednesdays and Saturdays in my area. As soon as they arrived we would scour the 'Houses for Sale' page and draw rings around the ones that seemed possible. During our phone calls we would discuss which ones were worth a visit. Enquiries at the local building society offices had revealed that although we would be able to borrow 90 to 95% of the cost of a newly-built house, an older terraced property was unlikely to qualify for more than an 85% loan. As we only had around £95 to put down as a deposit, any house costing over £1000 would be beyond our reach.

Although there were several estate agents in the Rochdale area, in the 1960's many people chose to advertise their houses privately in order to avoid paying agent's fees. This was a great advantage to us because having identified the houses we could afford, we would group them together in districts and travel to their location by bus. Of course, some houses barely warranted a second glance, being in a run-down locality or being so badly maintained that we would be unlikely to get a mortgage on them. When we came across a house that appealed to us, we would take a deep breath and knock on the front door.

It seems strange nowadays, when most house sale advertisements include the proviso 'Viewing by Appointment Only' to think that we could just turn up at an address and knock on the door. But as few private houses possessed telephones in those days, viewing could not be arranged in advance, so our arrival at someone's home – although unexpected – was usually accepted with good grace.

For several weeks our journeys through people's living rooms, kitchens and bedrooms became part of each Saturday afternoon's entertainment! Sometimes we were accompanied by a husband who would proudly point out all the improvements he had made since living there; sometimes by a wife who would tell us how convenient the property was for shops, schools and bus stops. Occasionally we would be welcomed by an older couple who would explain their reasons for wanting to move, tell us about the achievements of their children, invite us to make ourselves comfortable on the settee and provide us with tea and biscuits. At times, it was difficult to get away!

Many of the houses within our price range had an outside toilet and few inside facilities, but some terraced houses with high ceilings were able to have a tiny bathroom installed above the stairwell which housed a small washbasin, toilet and bath. These so-called 'conversions' were becoming very popular, as they enabled families to enjoy modern conveniences without having the expense of moving to a larger house.

One wet Wednesday evening early in January 1961, Anita and I met up and travelled to a district about two miles south of Rochdale centre, to view a property that I had seen advertised in Wednesday's edition of the Observer. It sounded just what we wanted – a terraced house with an open aspect to the front, a small yard with a toilet and coal store to the rear, and an inside 'conversion' containing a bath and washbasin.

As soon as we saw it Anita and I knew it would be just right for us. It was the second house in a long row of fourteen, just off the main road to Manchester. In front of the houses was a genuine stone-flagged pavement but the roadway itself had been unadopted by the council and was a stony, uneven dirt track. However, as it was a cul-de-sac, only the very few cars of the residents drove along it.

The property was built of Accrington stock brick and looked in very good condition. Inside there was a medium-sized front room with a vestibule and tiled fireplace, and a kitchen with a combustion stove in one corner and a cupboard under the stairs. The added bonus was a glass-roofed outhouse outside the back door which had been formed by bridging the space between the outside toilet (on the right) and the coal store (on the left). Upstairs were two good-sized bedrooms and a small 'conversion' over the stairs containing a wash basin and a short bath. The asking price was £895. We told the owners that we were very interested and arranged to return on the following evening with a firm decision.

On the next evening, having persuaded my father to accompany us to lend his support, Anita and I returned to make an offer on the house. Although we were pretty sure that we would be able to get a loan – providing the Halifax Building Society approved of the property – we also knew that if we were able to persuade the owners to lower the price a little, we would have less deposit to find. All three of us were shown over the house again, and at the end of our tour we successfully negotiated a price of £870, which satisfied the owners and filled us with delight. We now had a place to call our own, and everything was coming up roses!

We travelled our separate ways home that evening on cloud nine. After negotiations with the Building Society during the days that followed, we learned that the purchase of our new home was likely to be completed by the end of February. We knew that it would take us several weeks to do the basic painting and decorating which was all we could afford at present. But we relished the thought of getting on with it. We had a place to live. Now we could plan our wedding.

Chapter Seven

Planning the Wedding

Both Anita and I were inexperienced when it came to weddings. The only wedding I had ever attended was that of Auntie Annie who, at the mature age of 47, had married a widower. I was 15 years old and her wedding was a very quiet affair.

For her part, Anita had neither been a bridesmaid as a child nor a guest at a wedding reception as an adult. She had vague childhood memories of attending an Aunt's wedding shortly after the war ended, but that too had been a simple affair with no frills.

You could say that when it came to arranging weddings, neither of us had a clue!

However, as soon as the purchase of our house was confirmed, we began to plan our wedding. We decided that we wanted to be married in church, although at the time neither of us attended church regularly. Anita's mother was from a Roman Catholic background but had married a protestant. Anita had been a pupil at an Anglican Church school and had also attended Sunday school, later going forward for confirmation.

My mother was a life-long member of Greenhill Primitive Methodist Chapel in Littleborough. From early childhood I had been sent to morning and afternoon Sunday school every week, but I had rebelled during my teens and was now an agnostic. Nevertheless, we both thought that getting married in church was the 'right thing to do', so there were no arguments on that score – the only problem was where to have the ceremony!

From time to time over recent months Anita had attended the Sunday morning service at Cheetham Hill Methodist Church, about half a mile from where she lived, so she made an appointment for us to see the minister, the Reverend George Dolbey, to ask if he would be willing to marry us on Easter Saturday, 1st April, 1961.

At first Mr Dolbey said that he couldn't perform the ceremony on that day. He was a member of the Campaign for Nuclear Disarmament, which was very active at the time, and was intending to join a protest march – from Wethersfield or Aldermaston – being held over the Easter weekend. However, when he saw how disappointed we were, he very kindly decided that it *would* be possible for him to return home to marry us at 11.00 o'clock and then resume his protest march later in the day.

He told us that the church hall would be available for our wedding reception if we hadn't made any other plans and, as we hadn't, we jumped at the chance to book it immediately and thereby tick off another job from our list. As the wedding celebration would now be held on the same premises as the Service, any further difficulties of getting to another venue by car or coach were also instantly removed.

As we left the church that morning we felt happy with the all our arrangements. We were not to discover until the day of our wedding what a disastrous mistake we had made!

Having set the date, we began to compile our guest list. I had already asked Rod Ashman to be my best man, and our sisters Maureen and Pam were naturally chosen to be Anita's bridesmaids, but deciding who else we could ask was not an easy task. Although we had been saving hard since I started work, we did not have much money left to pay for a reception – only around £160 between us – so we were restricted to inviting close relatives. We knew that we could not afford to include our friends and hoped that they would understand. We thought perhaps that we could invite them for a meal when we were settled in our new home.

Almost everyone in my family lived in Littleborough, so it was easy to count heads and come up with a reasonable number. But Anita's relatives, from good Catholic stock in St. Helens, including all the cousins, added up to fifty or sixty! However, Anita's mother, who had left the Catholic fold twenty years earlier, persuaded us to omit most of them from the list, reassuring us by saying that they wouldn't want to come anyway.

In the end we settled on 25 guests in total – just the inner circle of close family members. Almost immediately the question arose as to how we were going to feed them! Not holding the reception in a hotel would mean that we would have to employ caterers. During the next few days Anita questioned friends and colleagues and was relieved to discover that certain large confectioners would supply everything that was needed for a wedding reception. One such firm was Robinson's of Piccadilly in Manchester and we paid them a visit, trying to hide our inexperience and appear knowledgeable and well informed.

Looking back, we must have been amongst the most naïve customers the manageress had ever dealt with. When we stated our business she gave a welcoming smile and embarked on a series of questions.

"What date and time is the Wedding Breakfast to take place? What is the address of the venue? How many guests will be attending? Will you require table cloths? Is there to be a colour scheme? Which menu would you require? Would you like us to provide the Wedding Cake? How many tiers would you like? Napkins? Crockery? Cutlery? Wine glasses?" and on and on… We stumbled through most of the answers, thinking on our feet, making instant decisions on questions that we hadn't even thought about until then.

During the conversation, it suddenly dawned on me that as the celebration was to take place in a Methodist church hall, we would not be allowed to serve alcohol. Although Anita and I rarely drank, and in fact had never even set foot in a public house together, the thought that we would have to be toasted by our guests with a soft drink suddenly seemed extremely odd. However, it was too late to do anything about it now, so we would just have to make the best of it.

We decided on a cold meal – basically a ham salad – which would be served with tea and bread and butter and followed by fancy cakes. The charge would be £1.00 per head – £25.00 in all. We selected a two-tier wedding cake, decorated with white lacy icing and topped with a posy of flowers.

As our conversation drew to a close, the manageress had one final question for us. "Have you engaged a photographer yet?"

We shook our heads. Although we hoped to have a pictorial record of the day, we had not got round to booking anyone to take photographs. The manageress saw an opportunity. She explained that she knew of an excellent, dependable photographer who worked in close co-operation with their firm and so, reassured by her words, we allowed her to make an appointment for him to call round to see us at Anita's home.

Two weeks later, we opened the front door to let in a well-dressed gentleman carrying a leather briefcase. Moments later Anita and I found ourselves leafing through the pages of a large padded album, staring glassy-eyed at countless pictures of well-heeled couples celebrating their big day.

Brides and bridesmaids had been photographed under trees on large expansive lawns; bridegrooms and best men, accompanied by clusters of male friends, had been captured tossing their grey top hats into the air; crowds of prosperous guests, surrounding the happy couple, had been pictured raising champagne glasses in a toast towards the camera.

It must have been apparent to our visitor that what we required was not quite in the same league. But in case he had not noticed that we were sitting in the tiny front room of a two-up two-down terraced house, we explained that we did not have a great deal of money to spend and was there something simpler we could choose? The photographer then produced his 'piéce de resistance'. He said that he could do us a very special deal. He had a new piece of equipment – a twin-lens camera – which with the aid of a special viewer could make each photograph appear three dimensional. He allowed us to look at some samples through the special 'binoculars', and we had to admit the effect was spectacular! The pictures were in full colour and had tremendous depth, everything appearing just as it would in real life. And when the photographer explained that, as a bonus, he would also supply two small conventional albums for our parents we decided to take the plunge. Then came the shock. The 3D photographs (with complementary viewer) were to be £1.00 each. 'How many would you like,' he asked, 'fifty?'

We eventually whittled the number down to twenty-five, but after he had gone we began to have serious doubts about the wisdom of our decision. Our photographs, although spectacular, would cost as much as the food for the reception, leaving us with only £100 with which to decorate and furnish our new home and to provide for any additional expenses!

One of the 'additional expenses', of course, was Anita's wedding dress! One Saturday morning – I think it must have been in February, 1961 – Anita and Pam met my sister Maureen in the centre of Manchester and all three went 'dress hunting'. Naturally I was excluded from this exercise and only saw the results of it on our wedding day.

They walked the length and breadth of Market Street, one of Manchester's busiest shopping areas in those days, searching for something that both bridesmaids-to-be could be happy with. Eventually, in a specialist shop tucked away round a corner, they decided on two pale primrose-yellow dresses with slashed necks and full skirts decorated with figured silk embroidery which suited both girls very well.

Then it was Anita's turn. The fashion of the day was for brides to wear ballerina length dresses and she quickly found one that pleased her. It was made of white satin and had a scooped neckline with a stand-up collar. The front panel was ruched and it was nipped in at the waist, which enhanced her figure. What is more, the price was right – just six guineas (£6.30).

Then came her moment of extravagance! Whilst searching for an appropriate headdress to go with it she came upon a delicate crown of imitation pearls and diamonds surmounting a bouffant veil, the height of fashion at the time. She fell in love with it immediately. When she asked the price however, she found it was more expensive than her dress, but encouraged by her bridesmaids she decided to throw caution to the winds. It was the right decision. On the day, her headdress looked wonderful and completed the outfit.

All that was necessary now was for the trio to be fitted with appropriate shoes, and as my father was the manager of Littleborough Co-operative Shoe Department at the time, this did not prove to be a major problem. A week later a visit was made to his shop – where they were given personal service – and all three found bridal shoes which enhanced their outfits perfectly.

Chapter Eight

Decorators!

When Anita and I turned the key in the lock and entered our new home for the first time in mid-February 1961 we were aglow with feelings of pride and elation.

The surveyor from the Halifax Building Society had given the property a clean bill of health, but having discovered a dark stain on the wallpaper beneath the front room window, he had stated that we must have that section of wall re-plastered. He told us that part of the loan would be held back until the job was completed. The previous owners had already told us about the damp patch. It had been due to a leaky window frame which had been put right by them the previous year, but nevertheless our surveyor insisted on the plaster being renewed and as I needed the mortgage I had no alternative but to comply!

I use the word 'I' here deliberately because Anita's name did not appear on any of the legal documents connected with the house. There was no joint ownership. Although she was old enough to get married and have a family, Anita was under the age of 21 and was not allowed to take out a mortgage. I took full responsibility for the loan, the maintenance of the property, and was liable to prosecution if any debts were incurred. Legally I was the sole owner of the house. I would tease Anita about this periodically – when I was sure there was nothing to hand which she could pick up and throw at me!

One of the first things we did was to fix newspapers over the windows to afford ourselves some privacy as we began to assess the task ahead of us. Three rooms in the house were in urgent need of fresh wall-paper – the front room (or 'lounge', as we called it), the kitchen and the front bedroom. My father knew of a good painter and decorator in Littleborough, George Howarth, and we arranged for him to call at the house to show us his 'pattern book' and to measure up the walls. Together we chose three of the contemporary papers which were highly fashionable at the time.

We picked a rural design for the lounge which portrayed scenes from village life, a paper with repeated clusters of cooking utensils for the kitchen and a Japanese-style pattern depicting pagodas, bridges over streams and sprigs of cherry blossom for our bedroom. Anita and I decided that to save money we could paint all the woodwork ourselves before George came in to finish the job by putting on the wallpaper. At this point Nellie, my favourite childhood Aunt, stepped in to help us out with the painting. After a full day's work in the mill, she and her friend Edith would travel to our new home by bus every evening for several weeks to wield a trusty paint brush. How we appreciated their help and support!

I soon discovered that I had many practical skills which to this point had remained dormant. As a child I had often helped my father at his hen-pen and had watched him as he fixed a padlock, wired up a lamp or repaired a wooden fence. I had seen him busy with household maintenance and general running repairs of all kinds within the home. Now I began to identify those hidden skills which had been passed on through his genes or learned at his knee.

There was a square porcelain sink fitted under the window in the kitchen which rested on two low walls of cemented bricks. These served their purpose, but were very unsightly. I decided that enclosing them within a timber frame might be a big improvement. I bought some lengths of wood and sheets of hardboard and with careful planning, constructed a cupboard with sliding doors, which we painted red and white to fit in with our kitchen colour scheme. The sink looked much better now, for not only were the ugly walls completely hidden but all the essential bottles, buckets, and dusters could be stored out of sight.

Flushed by my success, I looked around for further improvements which I could make. The cupboard under the stairs was dark and unpainted and had been used by the previous owners as a 'glory hole' – a cupboard into which all sorts of odds and ends were crammed. We thought this would make an ideal pantry, as it was entered from the kitchen and was fairly spacious, although it did have the disadvantage of diminishing in height the further one walked into it! I bought some lengths of wood and shelving brackets and began to fit it out to accommodate the pans, bowls, and jugs etc. we would be bringing with us when we moved in. Reconstruction completed, we added our new pantry to the list of areas needing a coat of paint.

Once the improvements to the fabric of the house were well underway, we began to think about the furniture and furnishings we needed. In the early 1950's a man called Cyril Lord had pioneered a new type of tufted carpet which was both inexpensive and very popular. We had seen it in the homes of newly married friends and Anita decided it would be just the thing for our lounge. The best rooms in our parents' homes had squares of carpet surrounded by linoleum, but we decided to indulge ourselves in the luxury of fully-fitted carpets.

Because of the method of manufacture, Cyril Lord carpets were not patterned. They consisted of a background colour with contrasting flecks all over it. We chose a red ground with black flecks for the lounge and a grey ground with black flecks for our bedroom. When they were fitted, they went right up to the skirting board – a dream come true!

An essential item on our list was a kitchen table with four chairs, and we bought a complete set from Pauldens in Manchester for a little over £11. The table was covered with red Formica and the beechwood chairs had red plastic seats. We ordered an electric cooker from a store in Rochdale – the only item we bought on higher purchase.

The only other piece of furniture we were certain to have was Anita's piano from home. Although it was quite elderly, it was made of polished walnut and was well loved by Anita, so it was to have pride of place in our newly carpeted lounge.

Of course our families were well aware of our financial situation so many of their wedding presents to us were for our home and were given to us in advance of the Big Day itself.

My parents' gift was a double bed and a suite of bedroom furniture consisting of a chest of drawers, a dressing table (identical to the chest but with a mirror) and a wardrobe. The furniture was made of veneered plywood, but was of the latest design – the two chests being supported by black tapering legs.

As we had no washing machine, Auntie Annie and Uncle Maurice gave us a Burco electric washing boiler, and Auntie Ethel and Uncle Charlie bought us a splendid kitchen cabinet, complete with sliding glass doors, a drop down bread-board, a glass shelf for cakes, a cutlery box and wire racks to hold packets and boxes fitted to the inside of the lower doors. It was a top-of-the-range piece of kitchen equipment – and of course it was red and white to fit into our scheme.

Anita's parents gave us a matching bedspread and eiderdown (this was long before the day of the duvet) and a set of cutlery. They also returned to us Anita's 'housekeeping' contribution for March so we had a few more valuable pounds to spend.

Everyone else bought us towels. For some unaccountable reason, almost all our other relatives and all our friends decided that a pack of towels would be just what we needed, so we ended up with cupboards full of them! It is true to say we did not need to buy another towel during the first ten years of our marriage.

There were a couple of rooms which remained unfurnished right up to our wedding day. The lounge, although carpeted, held nothing but Anita's ancient piano, and the back bedroom was left undecorated and completely empty – not even having a covering for the floorboards.

There were, of course, many other things we did not have, but as most other people of our age did not have them either, we did not feel deprived. Few people in those days had central heating and double glazing was unheard of, so temperatures would vary considerably as one moved from room to room.

We did not own a washing machine, so during the early months of our marriage all our laundry had to be done by hand – even sheets. For many years we did not own a 'fridge, so we had to be careful when storing food, particularly milk, which in summer seemed to 'go off' remarkably quickly. However, our outhouse – formed between the coal store and outside toilet and facing north, had a concrete floor and was very cool, so except in the warmest weather, we did not have too many problems.

Although at the time many people rented television sets, Anita and I considered this an unnecessary expense. However, Anita had always loved listening to the radio so we bought a brand new Bakelite set for just a few pounds and spent our evenings tuning in.

As the weeks passed, the empty terraced house that we had walked into on that cold February day was gradually transformed into our own cosy home. All our weeks of effort and fatigue had finally borne fruit. The newly papered and painted rooms seemed bright and cheerful and the wall-to-wall carpets felt wonderful underfoot.

Our efforts had been good for our figures too. Both of us had lost weight during the previous months, and we would have felt tired – even exhausted – if we had not been so buoyed up by the prospect of our imminent wedding and our future life together.

We left the house on the day before our wedding knowing that when we re-entered to it on the following afternoon, we would be man and wife. Our plan was to return home immediately after the ceremony – for we had no money left for a honeymoon.

Chapter Nine

The Ceremony

A week before the 'Big Day', Anita and I went to see Reverend George Dolbey at the Manse. He had said that he wanted to go through the Marriage Service with us to make sure that we understood the serious nature of the vows we were about to take.

Anita had already decided that she wanted to include the word "obey" in the ceremony – although it was no longer essential – and in return I would promise to endow her with all my worldly goods, which were very few at the time and seemed an extremely good swap for her total submission!

During the course of an hour or so Mr. Dolbey took us gently and sensitively through the service, explaining everything in detail and allowing us to comment or ask questions. At the end of the session he gave us the good news that he had talked with the organist and had persuaded her to reduce her fee!

The next few days flew by as we each packed up our belongings and began to move them into our new home. It felt strange to be hanging our clothes together in our shiny new wardrobe and deciding how we were going to organize drawer space. My mum had been secretly adding extra items to her weekly shopping list for several months and now proudly presented us with a carton of basic provisions such as salt, pepper, oil, sauces and so on. We were very grateful for the gift.

Soon the eve of our wedding was upon us. Neither of us had planned a pre-wedding knees-up with our friends. Stag nights and Hen parties were much rarer in those days and the idea hadn't even entered our heads. I had arranged for Rod Ashman to sleep at my parents' home that night, so bearing his best suit on a hanger and his highly polished shoes in a carrier bag, Rod arrived in his new acquisition – a green saloon car. The evening passed pleasantly as we exchanged news of old friends, joked and reminisced about college escapades and rehearsed what each of us had to do on the following day.

I awoke early next morning and on looking out of my bedroom window I discovered that the sky was grey and it was raining. It was a steady drizzle – just enough to wet the pavements but not enough to dampen my spirits. I was elated to think that in a few hours' time I would be a married man. I was overwhelmed by feelings of excitement tinged with a degree of apprehension.

Rod and I enjoyed a leisurely breakfast together (cooked by Mum) before returning to my bedroom to get into our wedding gear. We both wore conventional suits, complemented by new crisp white shirts, smart ties and cream carnations worn in the buttonholes of our left lapels. By half past nine all was ready, so with hugs and goodbyes from Maureen and Dad and a few tears from Mum, I got into Rod's car and we set off towards Manchester on my last journey as a single man.

When we got to the church, forty-five minutes before the ceremony was due to begin, the place was deserted! We wandered around the outside of the building for a few minutes without finding any signs of life. I thought the caretaker might be there at the very least. I hurried along to the adjacent church hall hoping to find the caterers laying out the wedding breakfast, but as I approached the closed doors I noted the absence of any delivery van parked outside them. My heart began to race and panic welled up in my chest. There was no-one there either – the caterers had not arrived!

Rod and I held a hasty conference and pooled the small change from our pockets. I ran along the road to a telephone box just a hundred yards from the church to make an urgent call to Robinson's Caterers asking them (in the politest possible way) what the devil they were playing at, and why no-one had turned up to provide our wedding breakfast? A motherly voice at the other end of the line calmly reassured me that everything was in hand. The van was on its way and by the time the ceremony was over and the photographs had been taken all would be ready.

I returned to the church to find that some of the wedding guests were already beginning to arrive, so Rod and I went in and took our places in the front pew. As I sat waiting for the ceremony to begin not only did I have the natural feelings of any nervous bridegroom but I also had the added pressure of wondering what on earth would happen if, by some chance, the caterer's van did not arrive on time.

* * *

Meanwhile, in Littleborough, a wedding car had picked up my parents and my sister and had driven them to Anita's home in Cheetham Hill, where Maureen, the chief bridesmaid, was dropped off, before my parents were brought to the church. My remaining relatives were driven over in relays in Uncle Charlie's Austin Seven that had been highly polished for the occasion.

I was not the only one experiencing pre-wedding problems. Things were not running smoothly for Anita either. Because our wedding was on Holy Saturday – the day after Good Friday when most businesses closed – Anita had to have her hair set on the previous Thursday. By our wedding morning it had broken free from the 'superglue' sprayed on it by the hairstylist and was 'doing its own thing'! One of Maureen's first duties on arrival was to rescue it and restore its 'freshness'. In an earlier incident, Anita had managed to cut the first finger on her right hand and a plaster had been applied to protect her white satin gown from the profuse flow of blood. Things were not going according to plan!

Having dropped off my parents at the church, the wedding car returned firstly to pick up Anita's mother and the bridesmaids and finally to convey the bride and her father to the ceremony. The problem was that no-one was paying particular attention to the timing of these trips, and the whole chain of events was running early. So although it is traditional for a bride to arrive at the church a few minutes late, when Anita and her father drew up outside the door they were ten minutes early!

They sat in the wedding car for a few minutes before posing for photographs on the church steps – fortunately the rain had cleared up – but even so it was barely eleven o'clock as they entered the church. The organ swelled to the notes of the Bridal March from Lohengrin and I turned to see the girl of my dreams walking down the aisle towards me. I thought she looked rather pale and wondered if her morning had been as fraught as my own.

* * *

Reverend George Dolbey guided us through the wedding ceremony and as we made our vows we spoke them out clearly meaning every word. I placed the gold band on Anita's finger but she did not give one to me in return as it was not the custom in those days. The organist played the hymns superbly and Anita and I sang enthusiastically, but each rendering was something of a duet as very little sound could be heard from the congregation!

After signing the register in the vestry we reappeared to process down the aisle to Mendelssohns's Wedding March and face a bank of photographers. Well, there were *two*! The senior partner was taking the coloured, three dimensional photographs with his twin-lens camera, whilst his assistant was taking the black and white photographs for our parents and guests.

When the last group photograph had been taken, the senior photographer came over to us and said, "Before the reception is over, I will be back with proofs of all the pictures we have taken, and your guests will be able to place orders for the ones they wish to buy before they leave."

This seemed like a good idea at the time – we did not realise that the arrangement would prove to be a problem.

Our party of twenty five guests followed us round the church building to the reception hall where I was relieved to see the caterer's van parked alongside the door. We led the group in and surveyed the scene. Let me describe it to you.

The church hall was high and spacious with a raised platform at one end containing a backdrop from 'Babes in the Wood'. To one side stood a rather battered baby grand piano. The plain wooden floorboards were marked out with a couple of a badminton courts and around the walls was a single line of grey tubular-steel chairs with canvas seats and backs.

At one end of this enormous room were half a dozen trestle tables arranged in the shape of a letter T. They were covered by white tablecloths and were set out with all the items of food that comprised our wedding breakfast. Anita and I were to sit in the centre of the top bar of the 'T' and before us stood the two-tiered wedding cake we had ordered on its silver stand. The plates had already been laid out for the guests and each contained slices of chicken and ham, lettuce, pieces of tomato, cucumber and hardboiled egg, and a serving of apple sauce and Branston pickle. In the centre of the table were cups and saucers, and several plates of small fancy cakes covered in pink, white or chocolate-coloured icing.

Before the guests took their seats, Anita and the bridesmaids posed for the photographers, sitting on the bare wooden floorboards looking up into the camera lens, and Anita and I pretended to cut the wedding cake together for one final shot by the creative duo before they dashed off to develop and print the film.

Photographs over, everyone came and sat at the table so that the feast could begin. Two uniformed ladies who had come with the caterer's van served us with tea, passed around various items of food and cut the lower tier of the wedding cake into small pieces to be taken away by the guests. Within what seemed a very short time the simple meal was over.

After speeches by the best man, Anita's father and me, the guests became separated into two groups which sat facing each other at either side of the large hall as the caterers cleared away the crockery and dismantled the tables. There was then a period of well over an hour when Anita and I flitted from side to side across the badminton courts talking first to the Stanleys and the visitors from St. Helens, and then to the Broome family from Littleborough. It had not occurred to us to provide background music or any other form of amusement for the guests and, as the two sides of the family were strangers to each other, they chatted to the people that they knew best – the ones with whom they had travelled to the wedding!

The reason for this prolonged delay was that we were all waiting for the return of the photographers, who had no doubt thought the reception would take several hours, so were in no particular hurry to return with the proofs. By the time they actually turned up, Anita and I were beginning to feel desperate – and the guests were showing signs of restlessness. However, as soon as the proofs were brought in, the guests gathered round, put in their orders and felt free to leave. Within a short time everyone had shaken us by the hand, thanked us for our invitation, wished us all the best for the future – and disappeared!

There were three of us left in the hall – Rod Ashman, Anita and myself. We made our way out to Rod's car and, as previously arranged, Anita and I sat in the back together whilst he chauffeured us home to our house in Tomlinson Street, Rochdale. There I carried Anita over the threshold – still in her wedding dress – and we said goodbye to Rod, who wished us all the best and drove off to his own home in Manchester.

Alone at last Anita and I were able to relax a little. We changed into more comfortable clothes, wandered around our new home in a state of euphoria and wondered how to spend the rest of the day. Although now free to consummate our marriage, we were both too shy to suggest retiring to bed immediately. So as it was still only 5 p.m. Anita began her wifely duties by making the tea!

Looking through the groceries we had bought on the previous Thursday, we made a careful selection from our store-cupboard and decided to dine on toasted cheese, crispy bacon, slices of bread and butter and a cream cake.

We finally retired to bed at around ten o'clock, happy to be together at last and looking forward to whatever the future might hold. What was more, as we had been married on a bank holiday weekend, we not only had the following day – Sunday – to enjoy together but also Bank Holiday Monday on which to celebrate our honeymoon.

Chapter Ten

Honeymoon

When Anita and I awoke on that Easter Sunday morning, we discussed how we should spend the first day of our honeymoon. As a child, I had always looked forward to Easter because over the Easter weekend a travelling fair would come to Hollingworth Lake – our local beauty spot – and set up its stalls and rides on a stretch of land by the Lake Bank. As it was a fine day I suggested that a trip to Hollingworth Lake might fill the bill and Anita readily agreed. However, before we were free to set off on our travels there were new tasks to be undertaken. I had to carry in some coke and do battle with the combustion stove in the corner of the kitchen, whilst Anita had to prepare breakfast and clear away the dishes afterwards.

In 1961, there tended to be a clear division of work and duties in society which was reflected in our marriage. I did not believe it was Anita's job to bring in the coal, light the fire or do any manual or repair jobs around the home, whilst in turn I never even considered turning my hand to ironing, preparing food or cooking meals.

These were the strong demarcation lines we had grown up with and seen within our parental homes. However, right from the start we began to modify the pattern in that we were always willing to help each other. Although I had taken the lead as we renovated the house, Anita had always been there to act as 'apprentice', passing tools, fetching and carrying and providing moral support, and conversely I was ready, when needed, to lend a hand with the housekeeping tasks within Anita's domain.

One job in which Anita needed my co-operation right from the start of our marriage was in the washing of clothes. Whilst we did not miss having a fridge or a telephone in the house (neither had been in our parental homes), laundry was a big problem as we had hardly any equipment to help us do the job. In 1961 my mother had an electric washing machine with electric rollers attached and Anita's mother had a wash tub and a large mangle in the back yard. We had neither! Although Auntie Annie and Uncle Maurice had bought us a Burco electric boiler as a wedding present – which was about the size of a tea urn and could be used for boiling small amounts of 'whites' – we had only the porcelain sink in which to wash our clothes. So one of our first purchases from our faithful local D.I.Y. shop was a small portable clothes mangle with 12" rollers that we could fix to the draining board of the sink with four large rubber suckers. It was by no means easy to wash sheets in the sink, and it certainly took the efforts of both of us to lift them out of the rinsing water and feed them through the tiny mangle we had bought. Cooperation and 'man-power' were essential!

However, on the day after our wedding, oblivious of the problems that lay ahead, we set off for Hollingworth Lake to join in the fun! The journey involved taking two buses and as the day was chilly Anita wore a warm blue and white hound's-tooth check coat and I wore my mackintosh, trilby and a pair of snazzy yellow gloves.

When we alighted from the bus we found the Lake Bank crowded with people intent on enjoying themselves on their holiday weekend. We pushed our way through the hordes of exuberant visitors until we reached the fair. Soon we were in the thick of it, surrounded by noise and excitement as people pushed forward, eager to get a seat in a dodgem-car, or a saddle on a merry-go-round horse. The roll-a-penny stall was doing great trade – although Anita and I had no luck – and the marquee loaded with slot machines was bulging to capacity.

We wandered through the fairground peering at all the stalls and smiling and waving to small children as they passed us again and again on the mini roundabouts. Towards the far edge of the fair we came across a coconut shy with fewer people around it, and I decided on impulse to test my skill and prove my worth as 'Husband and Provider'. I handed over a shilling (5p in today's money) and was given three wooden balls by the showman. My first throw missed completely, the second hit the target but failed to dislodge it but my third effort was successful! I proudly handed my prize, a (rather small) coconut to Anita and sauntered around the fair for the rest of the afternoon with the air of a knight who has just proved himself in a jousting tournament.

We returned home at teatime, tired after our day out but exhilarated by the experience of being a married couple. With a great deal of effort and the skilful application of a hammer and chisel, I was able to break open the coconut. And so we began our second evening together; sitting on our Cyril Lord carpet (we had no armchairs of course) in front of the coal-fire in the lounge, munching on pieces of juicy coconut flesh, as we tuned in to our new radio. Bliss! A little later, after banking up the combustion stove in the hope that it would remain alight until morning, we mutually decided on an early night.

During the remainder of our week's holiday from school we found lots to do. On Bank Holiday Monday we explored some of the lanes and byways within walking distance of our home. Even though we had chosen to live in an urban area, and could see fourteen mill chimneys from our back bedroom window, it was still possible to find several pathways quite close to home which were so peaceful and unspoilt that one could almost believe one was in the heart of the countryside.

We strolled along the canal towpath and watched moorhens and mallards swim in and out of the reeds with their young. We found stretches of open land alongside the railway embankment which had narrow pathways winding through them. On one such path we came across an old wooden shed which, although rather dilapidated and not within sight of any houses, was in fact a shop. There were displays of tinned food in the window and through the open doorway we could see a basic wooden counter with a plump, rather rough-looking woman standing behind it. On impulse Anita went inside and came out bearing a small tin of strawberries and a can of Plumrose cream (no sell-by dates in those days!) which we took home and ate for tea.

Later in the week, we visited my parents' home in Littleborough, and Anita's parents in Cheetham Hill – and it felt strange and yet empowering to be able to say goodbye to them at the end of the evening and to return to our own home. It had been great to have those few days together to grow accustomed to our newly married state, even if our honeymoon had been spent in Rochdale! Nevertheless, the holiday had passed all too quickly and soon we were preparing our briefcases ready for the return to work.

* * *

Although my journey to Alfred Street School was now the shortest it had ever been – taking just twenty minutes on one bus – Anita was not so fortunate. In order to be at Lower Kersal Junior School by 8.50 a.m. she needed to catch a bus to Manchester at 7 a.m. from the end of our street. Once in the city centre, she had a hurried ten-minute walk to Salford bus station from where she caught a second bus to Lower Kersal. If everything ran on time she would arrive at school by 8.45 a.m.

When school was over she had to undertake the journey in reverse order and did not arrive home until almost six o'clock. However, after a week or two she discovered an alternative and less hectic return route. She could take a bus from school to Victoria Railway Station in Manchester and pick up a train to Castleton Station which was only about a mile from where we lived. From there Anita had a comfortable walk home as it was mostly downhill.

After only a few weeks of her marathon journeys, Anita discovered that travelling so far every day was both exhausting and expensive. She decided to apply as soon as possible for a teaching post with Rochdale Education Authority. She would not be sorry to leave her first school. Working at Lower Kersal had not been a happy experience. There had been a serious shortage of books and basic equipment and there was no-one she felt able to turn to for professional advice.

The Local Education Authority rule is that teachers wishing to leave at the end of the summer term must hand in their notice by 31st May, so towards the end of that month Anita sent off the important letter and informed her head teacher of her decision. At the same time she applied for a post in Rochdale and within a few days was called for an interview with a senior education officer.

Anita must have done well in the interview, because as it ended the officer said that it was very likely they would be able to find a teaching post for her in Rochdale, but she shouldn't give in her notice until she had heard from them in a few days' time. At that Anita surprised him by saying, "I'm afraid I've already handed in my notice, and if you aren't able to give me a post in Rochdale, I'll have to apply elsewhere."

The officer raised his eyebrows. "Well, Mrs. Broome," he said, "I don't think you'll need to do that. You'll be hearing from us in a couple of days, and I'm sure the news will be positive." Three days later, Anita heard that she had been appointed to St. Peter's Junior School in Rochdale under the headship of Mr. Arnold Jones. This was a school in which she was to develop her teaching skills, make several lasting friendships and spend many happy years.

Chapter Eleven

Settling In

A nita and I were soon to learn that the local area in which we had chosen to live had its own characteristic name: Sudden.

A visitor might have had difficulty in defining its boundaries, for although long ago it had been a small hamlet set amongst fields a couple of miles from the town centre, by the time we moved in it was part of the huge urban sprawl connecting Rochdale with its neighbouring towns of Heywood and Middleton.

Nevertheless, a strong sense of local identity had persisted down the generations and most residents still referred to a section of the busy main road close to where we lived as 'Sudden Village'.

Our home in Tomlinson Street was within sight of the local parish church, St. Aidan's – a fine-looking building whose stone construction made it appear older than its years. It was sited on the main road from Rochdale to Manchester which ran through Sudden. Close by, a cluster of shops flanked either side of the road for a distance of about two hundred yards and this was the area known as 'Sudden Village'. They were all there – the butcher, the baker, the candlestick maker. There was Duckworth's, the family grocers, in competition with the local Co-op, and a number of small family businesses situated further along the road. There was our much-valued D.I.Y. and hardware shop owned by Ossie Hayhurst, who was always a source of helpful advice, and next door, the greengrocer's shop with its boxes of fresh fruit and vegetables spilling out onto the pavement. There was a fried fish and chip shop, a newsagent's, a sweet shop, the Post Office, two hairdresser's salons, a barber's shop, and two rival bakers and confectioner's which confronted each other from opposite sides of the road. It was a thriving community.

Across the un-adopted road in front of our house was a large playing field containing two football pitches. It provided for us the 'open aspect to the front' which had first attracted us when we saw the 'For Sale' advertisement.

This field belonged to Dunlop Mill, which had been constructed alongside the main Manchester to Rochdale railway line and was reputed to be the largest cotton mill in the whole of Lancashire, employing hundreds of people. Its various buildings stretched for about a mile beside the railway track, so the opposite end of it could legitimately be said to be in Castleton – the next centre of population along Manchester Road.

The Mill was more than just a workplace; for some it was the centre of their lives. It had a social club run by a committee, and all kinds of activities and excursions were planned for the families of workers. There was a comfortable bar in which members could relax, and a full programme of events took place throughout the year, including dances, concerts and Christmas parties. There was a sports club which had its own equipment and facilities (including a bowling green and tennis courts) and many workers were involved in playing for one or another of the Dunlop teams during summer evenings or over the weekend.

Sometimes, on a Sunday morning after breakfast, I would go upstairs and enjoy a grandstand seat at the football match which was taking place a few yards away across the road. This was an added bonus that I hadn't expected.

* * *

After our marriage, Anita had quickly adjusted to her new role of housewife and one of her weekly tasks was to do the shopping. Although I would usually accompany her to the shops to help carry the heavy bags, she had sole responsibility for deciding what food we bought and when we ate it!

59

Although we could have caught a bus into Rochdale centre to do our shopping in the market, it was far more convenient to walk 200 yards to buy our groceries from Duckworth's in the 'village'. This was before the days of self-service and customers had to wait at a counter to be served. Duckworth's manager, Mr. Greenwood was of the 'old school'. He always wore an impeccable white coat and flitted about his domain in a bird-like manner, keeping everything 'just so'. Butter, cheese and lard did not arrive pre-packed in those days. They were turned out of small barrels onto marble slabs and one's order had to be cut off and weighed out before being wrapped in greaseproof paper. Mr. Greenwood was an expert in this wrapping. His fingers would deftly crease and fold the paper and it would be presented to the customer as delicately as if it were a special Christmas present. But what impressed most were his good manners. Although he was in his seventies, he treated Anita – just twenty years old – with utmost politeness. He would advise her on what to buy and how to prepare it, he would pack her shopping bag and after she had paid the bill, he would scurry around from behind the counter to open the door for her with a courteous farewell. He was a perfect gentleman.

Just as Anita had thrown herself into the role of housewife, I became the property repairer and general handyman. Within months, we had decided that we urgently needed more storage space than that afforded by the bedroom furniture bought by my parents. Therefore I paid another visit to Ossie Hayhurst's hardware shop in the 'village' and asked for his advice on building a wardrobe – with a cupboard above – in an alcove in our bedroom.

Ossie spent a great deal of time explaining how I should make a frame and fix it in place, (checking that it was 'square' and not merely screwed to the walls which were unlikely to be truly vertical), and then advising me on the wood that I needed and the types of screws I should buy. When it came to the doors, which were to be made from plywood (chipboard hadn't been invented), he offered to cut them to size for me on his circular saw if I provided careful measurements and took full responsibility for their accuracy. Little by little Anita and I were becoming more confident in our roles. She was developing new culinary skills and after a few major hiccups (usually involving extremely tough or almost raw meat!) began to enjoy cooking meals. I too had several minor failures but gradually became more competent at woodwork and general household maintenance. And throughout all this, there were very few cross words between us.

* * *

Soon September arrived and Anita began working at St. Peter's Junior School in Rochdale under her new head teacher, Mr. Arnold Jones. He was jovial and helpful to all his staff members and was always ready for a good gossip! The atmosphere there was happy and relaxed and Anita began to enjoy her work.

She was given a first year junior class and felt comfortable with the other members of staff, several of whom became firm friends. Although Mr. Jones expected everyone to pull their weight he realised that people had lives outside the school walls and did not expect his teachers to stay on for long hours after school had closed.

"The home-time bell goes at half past three," he would say with a smile. "Anyone who is here after twenty to four needs their head examining!"

Because of his relaxed, yet supportive attitude, teachers were willing to spend their own time giving extra help to pupils, making their classrooms bright and attractive and taking football or netball matches on Saturday mornings. It is not always the hard task master that gets the best out of people.

I continued to teach in Harpurhey and in my second year the school became a true junior school, accepting children of both sexes. Dan Stewart moved and became head of a neighbouring primary school, and the head of the original Alfred Street Girls School, Nora Bottoms, became head of the amalgamated school. Although I had had some initial qualms about the changes, I soon found that I got on very well with her.

To mark its fresh start, the school was renamed Harpur Mount Junior School, and the children were given the option of wearing a basic school uniform (white skirt or shirt and green blazer) instead of just turning up in their everyday clothes. Knowing of my artistic ability, the head asked me to design a new logo and a blazer badge for the school, which looked very smart indeed when it appeared on the uniform blazers. In addition, knowing of my keen interest in reading, Miss Bottoms asked me to sort out and grade the combined reading books from the old boys' and girls' schools in order to produce a reasonably coherent scheme. I found it a rewarding task which soon had positive results.

By now Anita and I had settled down well. Our joint salaries totalled around £70 per calendar month, and we gradually bought things that made our life a little easier. One of my colleagues offered us a second-hand washing machine – with electric rollers attached – for £4, and we did not hesitate for a moment! We installed it in our outhouse, where there was already an electric socket. It still needed some effort on our part though, as it had to be filled with hot water by means of a rubber hose-pipe fixed to the taps in the kitchen and at the end of the wash and rinse cycles we had to drain the water off into the grid beneath our kitchen window. Even so, it was a great improvement on the porcelain sink and the portable mangle with its 12" rollers.

Married life was gradually becoming easier and we were very happy together.

Chapter Twelve

Moving On

Anita and I continued to live in Tomlinson Street for the next five years, gradually developing and improving our home. There was a patch of soil about eight feet long by six feet wide in what was really a back yard and that first summer Anita was delighted to see cornflowers burst into bloom just outside our back door. She had never before had a garden and began to take a lively interest in our little plot of land. At its far end stood an ancient un-used coal bunker against which a former owner had optimistically planted a Japonica shrub. In retrospect it was a pretty poor specimen but we thought it was wonderful.

I decided to plant a few potatoes, assuring Anita that they would 'break up the soil' – a phrase that I had heard my father use long ago in his hen-pen garden. I dug the soil, planted the tubers, and earthed up the stems as they began to grow tall, but to no avail for when we harvested our crop we discovered that they had all been eaten by slugs. It was my first attempt at self-sufficiency – I did rather better in later years.

We began to establish our place within our 'urban village'. Most people in the neighbourhood knew each other by sight if not by name. They lived side by side in the rows of terraced houses, or worked in the same factory or cotton mill, or perhaps met at weekends in shops, at church or in one of the two public houses.

In the same way we came to know the people in our street. Our next door neighbours to our right were baker Billy and his elderly mother Mrs. Windross, who was profoundly deaf, and to our left Jim and Lily Maskew, the proud owners of a Ford Anglia. We became friendly with the Jones family who attended the local Methodist church with their bright young lads, and the Halliwells who had one daughter already married and another at Grammar School. Fred Halliwell, in common with many northern working men, had a wry sense of humour and a clever turn of phrase. Whenever someone suggested doing something that he considered a waste of time – in particular supporting the lowly Rochdale Football Club – he would protest by saying, "I'd rather walk up Sudden wi' a nail in mi shoe!"

Shopkeepers in the 'village' began to know us by name as we became regular customers and they were always willing to give advice, when asked. The butcher sorted out Anita's problems with the weekly joint, and the local builder helped me to select an appropriate cowl for our combustion stove chimney, thus saving us from being poisoned by the noxious fumes that periodically filled the kitchen.

Nowadays it would be said that Sudden was a happy, close community in which to live.

In our third year of marriage we took the bold step of buying a black, second-hand A35 car. It had been owned by the brother-in-law of an old school friend. The relative was a country man from Somerset, and for some undisclosed reason he had been in the habit of carrying chickens in it, so our first job was to remove the straw! Brian, the old school friend, generously offered to teach me to drive, so within a few months we were able to visit our families by car in a fraction of the time our journeys had taken to date. The next step was for me to teach Anita how to drive, which of course I did with supreme patience. She only got out of the car in a fury once and it wasn't the end of our wonderful relationship! Anita turned out to be a star pupil and passed her test first time.

However, during the mid-1960's Sudden began to change. Estates of new houses were built on fields adjoining our urban village. Each new house or bungalow had a back and front garden and a driveway which separated its occupants from neighbouring houses so it was less easy to befriend the people in one's street.

The rise of the motor car brought changes too. In the late 1960's, a network of motorways was being built throughout Britain, and two miles south-east of Sudden the construction of the Cross-Pennine route, the M62, was in progress.

The Rochdale and Oldham take off point (Junction 20) needed roads to enable traffic to move quickly to the centre of both towns, and so the A627M link road was built. On its Rochdale side the road fed a constant stream of vehicles through Sudden, and it soon became obvious that the existing Manchester Road – unchanged for decades – could not handle the increased traffic. A new wide dual carriageway was needed.

Plans were drawn up and within months the entire geography of the area was altered as a new dual carriageway and a gigantic roundabout split Sudden in two. Everything began to change. The shops on the old road lost most of their passing trade, and many had to close. The final blow came when a large Tesco store opened alongside the new dual carriageway. This finished off those businesses which had so far held out against the odds. Our community of Sudden – riven in two by the planners– had lost its heart, its culture and almost all of its facilities.

Alongside these physical changes the economy of the area was changing too. The local cotton industry had fallen into decline as cheaper imported goods were undercutting those produced in Britain. All around us the Rochdale cotton mills were closing, to be demolished or replaced by smaller business units which employed far fewer people. A generation of skilled workers was unemployed and the morale of the people dropped. It was the end of an era and life for many necessitated moving on.

At around this time several of our friends, both old and new, were starting families and, hearing about their child-rearing adventures, Anita had become 'broody'. But although we loved each other dearly, our efforts to produce a baby were not successful. We soldiered on for a couple of years but eventually, by now somewhat distressed, Anita decided to go for tests to see if there was a problem.

She came back from the examination with a clean bill of health – everything was as it should be. So fairly reluctantly I volunteered to follow her, convinced that I would get a similar outcome. However, when I was called back to hospital for the results of the tests the doctor had some sobering news. He told me that I had a very low sperm count and that conception was extremely unlikely. My problem was possibly a result of mumps which I had had when I was a child. There was little that could be done about it, although there was a very slight chance that an operation might improve things a little.

I think I must have found this information particularly traumatic as I cannot recollect returning home and telling Anita the news. But thinking back now, I realise what a tremendous blow it was for her. She very much wanted to have a child of her own but, married to me, this was not going to be possible. During the next few months we wondered if there was any way we could overcome the problem – but never once did Anita say anything hurtful about my predicament or attach blame to me for our situation.

Eventually, we began to explore the idea of adoption together and having had all the necessary medical examinations and visits from Social Services prior to making our application, we sent off the forms to Ashton-under-Lyne Adoption Society requesting that we be considered as adoptive parents.

Exactly nine months after our application was accepted we were notified that a little boy had become available and we hurried down to their offices to see our 'new' baby who was just ten weeks old. Of course we had prepared for his arrival by buying a pram, cot, nappies, etc. but we were given no help or advice which we would have received if Anita had given birth herself. So for the next few weeks we were on a steep learning curve! However, delighted to be parents, we bonded with little David immediately and happiness reigned supreme.

About two years later we decided that we would like a baby girl to complete our family. We felt sure we would be accepted again by Ashton-under-Lyne Adoption society, but there was a snag. If we intended to adopt a baby girl there was a rule that she had to have her own bedroom – not share it with her little brother – and of course our house in Tomlinson Street had only two bedrooms.

We had a decision to make. We had lived in our first home for almost six years and had been happy there, but now we needed another bedroom. In addition we seemed to be surrounded by change. Our neighbours -

the Jones family – had announced that they were moving to a house on the other side of town and the Maskews, who were almost surrogate grandparents to their boys, felt unsettled by the loss and decided to move on too.

So on 5th November 1966, after searching for several weeks for a new home that contained an extra bedroom and a garden for our prospective family, we closed the door of No 9 Tomlinson Street for the last time. But strange as it may seem, we couldn't bring ourselves to leave Sudden. We moved into one of the new semi-detached bungalows that had been built on the land belonging to Marland Hill Farm. It was a corner site with a large, south-facing garden, just made for little ones. We were now able to adopt a baby girl and very soon our daughter, Lisa came along. She was very tiny – only six weeks old – but now we were more practiced at dealing with little ones. So we now had a new home and our family was complete.

PART TWO

An Altered Consciousness

Chapter Thirteen

New Challenges

In early November 1966 Anita and I moved into our new house and gradually began to transform it into our ideal home. There was quite a lot of decorating to be done. We were the second owners of the house – the young couple before us had moved in when it was newly built and had lived in it for less than two years. The husband was a commercial traveller and they had done very little in the way of improvements.

We also had a large garden to design and plan. Although south facing it was full of established weeds and quite unkempt and neglected. So for the first two or three years we were fully occupied, but extremely happy, working away at creating a family home.

Little David and Lisa grew into toddlers and had lots of space in which to run and play, and we all made regular visits to our parents homes in Littleborough and Cheetham Hill, so the children could keep in touch with their grandparents. Eventually David and Lisa were enrolled into the local Primary School and settled in well.

The years rolled by and we were a happy family unit. The children made good progress at Marland Hill Primary School, and both Anita and I provided a weekly 'taxi service' to take David to guitar lessons and Lisa to ballet class.

Anita gained a part time job at All Souls Primary School in Heywood under the headship of Miss Greenhalgh, initially working two afternoons a week and eventually two days a week.

I succeeded in getting 'Head of English Department' in a large Primary School in Rochdale, and just one year later gained the Deputy

Headship of Blackshaw Lane Primary School in the neighbouring district of Royton.

It turned out to be a rather traumatic appointment as the Head of the school was already seriously ill when I took up my post. Sadly he died within a few months, leaving me in charge of the school until the end of the year.

Interviews to appoint a new permanent head teacher took place towards the end of the year and of course I applied for the post. When the shortlist was drawn up I was pleased to find that I had been included. I knew that in a situation like the present one most short-listing panels would include the acting head out of courtesy, but even so my hopes remained high.

Interviews were held one evening after school, and as I sat in the staff room waiting to be called in, it dawned on me that my lack of experience put me at a grave disadvantage. Most of the other candidates had been deputy heads for a number of years and two of them were already head teachers of smaller schools. In the event, my interview went reasonably well, and the panel expressed their appreciation of the work I had done during my acting headship, but when the educational advisor came out at the end of the evening it was to call in another candidate.

When he re-emerged, having accepted the post, we all shook his hand and congratulated him warmly. But whilst the other candidates were returning home with feelings of disappointment, mine were of apprehension. For I knew that when the next academic year began, the man whose hand I had just shaken would be the decision-maker, whilst once again I would be the deputy.

The new head teacher was a tall, middle-aged man with mousey hair, a ready smile and a Yorkshire accent. He changed many things when he came into post – the time of the morning assembly, the way children came in from playtime, even the abandonment of the school bell to signal breaks or the end of lessons.

In a conversation around Christmas time, he brought up a subject that made me think.

"How long is it since you left college?" he asked.

"Oh... about 14 years I think. Why?"

"You might be due for a long course," he said. "You had a particularly difficult time last year and if you apply for secondment now, the *powers-that-be* might view it quite sympathetically."

That evening, I talked the matter over with Anita. Local authorities released a number of teachers each year on full pay to allow them to complete a course of approved study at a college or university.

Anita was very encouraging.

"You've got nothing to lose," she declared. "Just fill in an application form and see what happens."

I needed no further encouragement. I scoured the educational press for suitable courses, seeking out those aimed at developing teaching skills to be used with slower learners.

I had always had a soft spot for those who did not find learning easy. As a child I usually found memorizing lists of names, countries or dates difficult – yet this was the quality which tended to earn high marks in examinations. On the other hand, I was very good at remembering *processes* or *ways of doing things* – making me good at art, woodwork and other practical tasks – but these tended to be less well regarded. They were not useful in passing most school tests!

So it is not surprising that in my search for interesting courses, I began to focus on those designed to help teachers understand and work more effectively with disadvantaged children.

One morning I came across an advertisement for a course leading to a Diploma in Compensatory Education at Didsbury Teacher's Training College in Manchester. It seemed to be exactly what I was looking for. It was designed to explore ways of helping pupils who were performing significantly below expected levels in reading, mathematics, and other subjects. What is more, it was being held at the college at which I had initially trained as a teacher and met Anita – although its name had now been upgraded to the grander-sounding Didsbury College of Education.

With Anita's encouragement I sent off to the college and the Local Authority for the required forms, completed them, and returned them to the appropriate departments within the week.

Soon I was called for interview at Didsbury and within days heard that I would be offered a place on the course, provided the Local Authority granted me secondment. A few weeks later I received a letter from the Divisional Education Officer stating that I would be given a year's secondment conditional upon Didsbury College of Education accepting me as a suitable student. Both pieces of the jigsaw fitted together perfectly. I knew that in a few months' time I would be freed from classroom responsibilities to plan my future direction and to explore in detail the concept of Compensatory Education.

* * *

Anita was as pleased as I was that I had gained access to my chosen course, but around this time there was a health issue which was causing us both concern. It had begun in the early years of our marriage. About four years after our wedding Anita – still in her mid-twenties – had been alarmed to discover that the joints of her arms and legs were becoming stiff and sore and beginning to swell. A persistent ache at wrists and shoulders made her feel unwell and began to keep her awake at night. Eventually, she visited the doctor. A succession of tablets was prescribed over the following weeks, and after some time the illness had subsided and disappeared.

But now we were settled in our new home and had become parents it returned with crippling severity and was diagnosed as Rheumatoid Arthritis. Anita found herself unable to grip door handles, lift heavy saucepans, or even dress herself. The gnawing pain in the joints of her arms and legs coupled with increasing immobility, once again drove her to seek medical help. The doctor prescribed two months complete rest, and a variety of tablets.

Eight weeks of inactivity, and the absorption of several hundred tablets into her bloodstream led to little improvement. She became allergic to aspirin, and was still in pain. She also became depressed.

The G.P. decided that more specialist help was required. He referred Anita to the Rheumatism Clinic at Manchester Royal Infirmary.

After several visits and numerous tests, the illness was brought under control. For three years, with the continuous help of a number of drugs, Anita had been almost back to normal. She had learned to tolerate a certain level of pain, and had accepted that she could not lift or manipulate heavy objects. With resignation she realised that she was unlikely to recover from the illness, but was thankful that she could lead a relatively normal life.

* * *

Also at around this time, Anita and I began to explore the idea of buying a small touring caravan. It would enable us to travel to a variety of places for holidays and what is more we would always know what the accommodation was going to be like when we got there!

But there was a problem – we had a very small car. Then we discovered the 'Sprite Sprint', advertised as an especially lightweight and narrow bodied caravan – not much wider than a family car. The advertisements said it could be towed by a mini!

We enquired a little further and discovered that it would sleep four – two adults and two children – and was very compact, even possessing a toilet compartment.

So in the early 1970s, after a little more research, we finally took the plunge and bought the Sprite Sprint touring caravan. I had made a parking place for it adjacent to our detached garage so we could go inside it whenever we wished. In fact I seem to remember we all had a 'practice sleep' in it one night even before it left our drive! It seemed to fill the bill exactly. When on holiday we did not have the restrictions of staying in a hotel and yet we had most of the comforts of home and could arrange menus and meals as we wished. We had a few 'trial runs' to caravan sites close to home, and then began to venture further afield.

We joined the Caravan Club and began to seek out their sites wherever we went. We found the facilities much to our liking with electric link-up points (from which we could run the fridge and the lights) and central toilet and shower blocks which were always clean and well-kept. And it was whilst we were staying on one of these sites in 1976 that an event took place that was to change the direction of both of our lives.

Chapter Fourteen

A Performance

Britain was enjoying its best summer for years. The sun moved daily across a clear blue sky and we were on holiday in York in our touring caravan. We were really enjoying our stay. Anita had been captivated by the history of the city and spent hours studying the mini-guide and planning walks which took in as many crumbling ruins as possible.

Our children, David and Lisa, aged eleven and nine, were enjoying themselves too. The Caravan Club site in York is next to Rowntree Park, so they had plenty of room in which to run and play. Lisa had a daily session on the swings and roundabouts, and David and I played endlessly with a frizbee, flicking it to each other like a miniature flying saucer across the open expanses of grass.

We first saw the notice on Thursday afternoon as we were exploring the streets around the Minster. That morning we had visited the National Railway Museum and looked admiringly at the giant locomotives gleaming under their new coats of paint. We had walked around the city via the ancient walls, and had viewed the majestic Minster from all angles. We had been fascinated by the little huddled shops in the Shambles, and had wandered through the busy open market where everything from cheese to china was on sale. Now we were strolling along the sunlit streets enjoying the warm sunshine and watching the hundreds of foreign tourists hurrying to and fro between the places of interest. Then we saw the notice. It was pinned to a wooden board, leaning against the wall of an old stone church, in the shadow of the Minster.

"Perhaps that's somewhere we could go this evening," suggested Anita, nodding in the direction of the board. I didn't read it carefully – to this day I can't remember the wording – but I gathered that there was some sort of open-air concert due to take place that evening in a courtyard near Stonegate. Anita took in the details, and I just nodded in agreement. I thought it might be something different to do after tea instead of just wandering around looking in shop windows.

The children, who never cared much for our evening walks – except to the fish and chip shop – seemed quite enthusiastic. So it was decided that the concert, or whatever it was, would be graced by our presence at 8.00 p.m.

* * *

When we got there, they were still putting out the chairs. We were too early of course, but then Anita likes to arrive everywhere early. Anyway, it didn't really matter because it was a warm, sunny evening. The courtyard was on the site of a twelfth century house, the oldest dwelling place in York. We stood for a while looking around at what was left of the stonework, trying to identify features of the ancient building, but as people began to come into the courtyard we settled ourselves on the front row of chairs so that the children could get a good view of the proceedings.

"What an ideal place this is for an outdoor entertainment", I thought. The stone walls of adjacent buildings flanked three sides of the area and on the fourth side, set back a little, was a hall with a door that opened into the courtyard. Several rows of chairs had been placed across one half of the space, leaving room in front for the 'action' to take place. The audience entered through a narrow passage at the rear which led from Stonegate. As I looked round, I saw that more people had now come in and the chairs behind us were beginning to fill.

A few minutes before eight o'clock a group of about seven young men and women appeared at the door of the hall. They were wearing old jeans and an assortment of cotton tops. One of them was sporting a wide-brimmed straw hat, and at least two were carrying guitars. They disappeared down the passageway into Stonegate, and two minutes later the sound of their voices floated back to us, accompanied by the firm beat of rhythm guitar. At the same time, two young men set about arranging the 'stage'. They erected a light canvas screen across one corner of the area and began to put various 'props' behind it – a sweeping brush, a scarf, a bowler hat and other small items.

All at once the trickle of people coming up the passage from Stonegate increased to a steady flow. Soon all the chairs were taken. The two stage managers, having completed their task, disappeared into the hall and, seconds later, reappeared carrying two stacks of chairs. Hurriedly they passed these to the people who were standing at the rear. A new back row was formed – and then another. Eventually, as there was no more room for chairs, several people remained standing in a group at the back, effectively blocking the passageway. One thing was certain – whatever sort of show this was going to be, it was going to play to a capacity audience.

The song that was being sung in Stonegate was coming to an end. I had been so interested in the problems of accommodation at the rear of the courtyard that I'd not really been listening to the musical strains floating in from the distance. Now, all at once, the tune impinged itself upon my brain. It was a catchy, rhythm-filled version of 'Jesus loves me, this I know'. My heart sank. "Oh hell," I thought. "It's a religious meeting!"

* * *

The first sketch was very amusing. It was hard to believe that the players were amateurs. They were so enthusiastic and uninhibited, that in spite of myself I was soon laughing with everyone else. The action was concerned with Man's downfall. A good-looking young man was seen succumbing to every temptation under the sun. Another young man, with an exaggerated stoop and wearing a long grey beard played the part of his father, and tried to give him good advice – but to no avail. In each

77

succeeding scene the 'son' became in turn proud, vain, lustful and lazy and at last inevitably came to a sticky end.

A musical interlude followed. In a clear, resounding voice a girl with a guitar sang a song I'd never heard before. I found myself impressed by her sincerity and directness. Then there was another sketch with more comedy and laughter. Scene followed scene, and over an hour later everyone was still enjoying the show.

The sun was low in the sky, and a chill had crept into the night air when the performance drew to a close. A young, bearded man with dark eyes, holding a bible in his hand, stepped to the front. "Here it comes," I thought. "Now for the religious bit."

He said that he hoped we'd enjoyed the performance. The people we had seen performing were Christians and they believed that Jesus wanted to come into our lives, too.

He went on to say, "If you have ever bought a new clock and put it in your bedroom, for the first few nights the tick seems really loud. In fact, it is so persistent that it may even keep you awake. But as the days go by you get used to it, and after a time you don't even notice it."

"God's like that," he said. "He is knocking at your door right now, but if you continue to ignore the knocking, the sound will seem to diminish and you will not hear it." Then he gave a general invitation to the audience. "Coffee is being served in the hall, right after my closing prayer. Come and have a coffee and a chat with the people who have been entertaining you."

It was at this point that I declared it was way past the children's bedtime. I think Anita would have stayed for coffee, but she didn't get the chance.

"Come on," I said briskly. "Let's get back to the caravan. It's getting late."

I led the way purposefully down the passage into Stonegate. Glancing round, I could see two young women coming from the hall into the courtyard carrying trays of steaming coffee cups. They began to hand them to the groups of people who were standing around chatting happily together.

As we set out towards the caravan site I thought to myself, "It may be comforting for those who need it, but it's not for me!"

Chapter Fifteen

An Unexpected Gift

It was really quite surprising the way I kept thinking about God. I'd be walking along the street looking into shop windows or driving to work in the car when suddenly I'd find myself thinking about God. I didn't believe in him of course – I'd got past all that years ago.

As a child I'd been sent to Sunday school twice every Sunday. Primitive Methodist. Morning at 10.30. Afternoon at 2.30. Regular as clockwork. Boring.

Although it did liven up for a time. At the end of the Second World War three young airmen returned from battle and became our Sunday school teachers. Following the opening hymn and prayer, we formed groups for bible class. At this point boys and girls were separated, probably as a disciplinary measure. I've no idea how the girls spent *their* time, but for the boys our 'bible class' was a journey into adventure. Every week, despite his best intentions, our ex-fighter pilot succumbed within minutes to the adoration and shrewd questioning of his group of nine and ten years olds. We would listen eagerly to the descriptions of his plane, and the night flights he had made. We would gasp as he described some exciting incident – but we groaned and protested when he tried to interest us in a story about Jesus. Eventually, we persuaded him to read a 'Biggles' book to us as a weekly serial, and for a time this made Sunday school tolerable, if not enjoyable.

Of course, it was too good to last. One weekend we were disturbed to hear that our hero had decided to be a Sunday school teacher no longer. His conscience had been too much for him. He had known in his heart that Biggles was not the correct diet on which to feed his young charges, so he had handed in his resignation.

From then on, things deteriorated rapidly. The Superintendent had felt it his duty to take us under his wing where by degrees we were spiritually suffocated. For the next year or so we trudged solemnly through bible story after bible story until I could stand it no longer. I angered my parents, I distressed the Superintendent, and I stopped going to Sunday school.

* * *

I was surprised to receive the gift. It was Saturday morning and Anita had returned from her weekly shopping trip into Rochdale and handed me a brown paper bag.

"I've bought you a present," she said.

It was November 1976. The day was cold and memories of the long hot summer were fading fast. Periods of torrential rain were beginning to refill the depleted reservoirs, and our holiday in York was just a memory.

I unfolded the paper bag and removed its contents. A book. I looked at the title: 'Good News for Modern Man'. It took a few seconds for the penny to drop.

"It's a bible!" I said, rather non-plussed.

"I thought it would come in handy for you to use at school."

"Thank you," I replied. "It probably will."

I don't know if the surprise showed on my face, but it was a most unexpected gift. Anita knew I was an agnostic and had never shown any real interest in religion since our marriage. In any case, our house was full of bibles. Small ones that had been given to me as Sunday school prizes. Large ones that had been handed down from great aunts and uncles, and a small, black, leather-bound one in a box that Anita had bought at the age of sixteen. I had never opened any of them in fifteen years of marriage.

I leafed through the pages of this modern version of the New Testament with simulated interest. The first thing that struck me was that it was comprehensible. I read through a couple of paragraphs at random and discovered I could actually understand them.

As a child I had always found the bible completely baffling. Of course, I had understood bible stories when they were told to me by adults, but the 'Good Book' itself had always been a mystery. I had found the use of language, grammar and phraseology so different from modern English that I had neither the patience nor the inclination to read more than three verses at any one time.

The second feature I noticed was a reading plan at the back of the book. The introduction to it read:

"The bible is mostly presented to us in unconnected bits. Readings in church are often chosen in a random manner, and if people dip into the bible many just read where it falls open. Yet the bible is intelligent writing by intelligent men written for real situations under the inspiration of God. Its real benefit comes when we approach it like this and read it all in a sensible way, looking for God to speak to us as we read.

The reading plan is designed to help you get to know the whole New Testament in one year in this clear, new translation. Each day's reading is only about one and a half pages and follows the clear section headings in Good News for Modern Man!"

The words appealed to me. I have always been fascinated by tick lists and logical progressions. When we bought our first car, the elderly black A35 which needed servicing every 1,000 miles, I got tremendous satisfaction from ticking off the jobs in the service book as I completed them. I found myself attracted to reading this book right through.

Moreover, since the holiday in York I had had a vague awareness within me of a spirituality that I had not known before. It was as though deep inside me a switch had been turned on. Outwardly, physically, there was no change, but inwardly there had developed an awareness and a searching that needed to be satisfied. Somehow I felt that reading the book might help to clarify matters for me.

I suppose I should have found it remarkable that it was *Anita* who bought the New Testament for me, but such an idea did not cross my mind. Looking back now, it seems a most unlikely gift for her to have chosen. After all, twelve years earlier Anita had declared herself to be an atheist!

Anita had been twenty-four years of age when she had decided there was no God. We had been married for four years, and it had been a tremendous relief for her to be able to make that decision! She could now look forward to a brighter future in which she no longer felt oppressed, judged and threatened by punishment. She felt free at last and was glad to be so!

Just three months into our marriage our local G.P. had had to make an appointment for Anita to see a psychiatrist. She had begun crying uncontrollably, and was desperately afraid that some terrible accident was going to happen to me.

The psychiatrist decided that Anita's concept of God was a significant cause of her problem. During her adolescent years she had become convinced that God had been critically watching her every move and observing how she was unable to keep his rules. Her failures and deficiencies had all been recorded. She had become terrified that now she had married, he would prevent her from enjoying what she did not deserve – a happy, contented life and a lovely home of her own.

As weeks went by Anita found herself living on a knife-edge of anxiety, afraid that the people she loved and the things she cared about most would be snatched away from her. God might act at any moment to deprive her of the undeserved joy she had found in marriage.

* * *

Anita's treatment had been long, but the psychiatrist had been thorough. He had not prescribed any medication but had helped Anita to think through the ideas that had developed during childhood. Her ideas about God had totally destroyed her self-worth, so after many months of thought, self-examination and heart searching, she had managed to discard them.

The misconceptions coincided with her attendance at church. When she was twelve, Anita had begun to take an interest in Sunday school. Until then she had attended spasmodically but found it fairly boring.

However, when she was fourteen her visits to Sunday school and church became more regular, and her involvement with the church gradually deepened. She enjoyed the singing, and the ritual of the services satisfied an inner need. At sixteen she had been enlisted as the Sunday school pianist and was given the responsibility of caring for the three and four year olds in the 'baby class'. She enjoyed the approval of the adult leaders, pleased that they considered her conscientious and reliable.

It was around this time Anita began to experience deep inner feelings of inadequacy. She found it difficult live up to the high standards of behaviour she set for herself. She began to pray regularly for forgiveness and within a short time became trapped in a ceaseless round of self-condemnation, repentance and re-dedication. Although she was regarded as a popular young church member in an ageing congregation, she began to carry around within her a burden of guilt from which she could not free herself. Over the years, the problem developed causing depression and a total lack of self-confidence.

Now, at last, she had been liberated through psychotherapy and welcomed atheism with open arms.

Chapter Sixteen

A Coincidence?

I found that I actually enjoyed reading 'Good News for Modern Man'. Every evening before settling down to sleep, I would prop myself against the pillows and read the prescribed section, ticking off the appropriate square in the reading plan. Sometimes I would even read two or three day's episodes at one go, the words leaping from the page with a total reality that I found compelling.

The more I read, the more respect I had for Jesus' abilities, as he dealt so capably with those around him. The depth of his compassion for the sick and the poor, and his mastery of every potentially difficult or dangerous situation filled me with admiration. On several occasions I found myself laughing aloud at the plight of the Pharisees who, after carefully planning to trick Jesus, found themselves thwarted by his sheer intelligence and deep understanding of their nature.

As the weeks went by, the whole story of Jesus' life unfolded afresh before me. The miracles, the teaching, the betrayal, the crucifixion and the resurrection seemed aglow with a newness which made me feel as if I had never heard of them before.

I went on to read about the early Christians; how at Pentecost they had received the Holy Spirit with an outburst of confusion and joy; how they journeyed around the Mediterranean facing difficulties and persecution; and how they remained utterly dedicated to following Christ and spreading the gospel.

The story satisfied me. I was aware that the events had taken place two thousand years ago, but the truths expressed felt totally relevant to the present day.

There was no doubt in my mind that Jesus had actually lived – and that he had possessed a dynamic personality and been a great leader. Of course, he couldn't have risen from the dead, I realised that. And he certainly couldn't be alive today. That just didn't make sense. But he had been a most remarkable man.

* * *

It was Anita who began the conversation one night late in December as we prepared for bed.

"Promise me that you won't laugh if I tell you something," she said with some embarrassment.

I promised. Anita sat on the bed wondering how to begin, and I stopped undressing and looked enquiringly across the room at her. I had had a faint suspicion for some time that her thoughts had been running parallel to mine, so I was only mildly surprised when she said,

"Something curious has been happening to me recently. I keep thinking about religion all the time. I can't seem to get God out of my mind."

I had been right. Completely separately, and with no conversation between us on the matter, we had both begun to consider the purpose of life, and our ponderings had brought us to reconsider the idea of God.

Anita looked across the bedroom, waiting for my reaction.

"That's really strange," I replied hesitantly, "because the same thing has been happening to me."

As I said the words, I felt suddenly apprehensive. My mind went back to those early days of our marriage when life had been difficult for both of us. Scenes replayed in my mind of Anita crying uncontrollably and myself unable to say or do anything to make her feel better.

The mere fact that Anita and I seemed to be developing a new 'religious awareness' was a worry and an embarrassment to me. I was repelled by the idea! We were nicely settled now – and it hadn't been easy.

Our arrival at a happy marriage had been the result of a long and sometimes painful journey, but in the end we had won through. Surmounting our difficulties had welded us together as a couple, and now we were able to discuss personal, intimate matters of every kind. Religion could add nothing to our lives. In the past it had caused us nothing but trouble!

As I got into bed there were two concerns on my mind: Anita's mental health and my own vulnerability in the situation. I didn't want to discuss, or even acknowledge, my own deepening interest in Christianity. I made a firm and positive decision to put it to one side. I reasoned that if God *did* exist something would eventually happen to prove it.

Anita was a little surprised at my reaction, but she could see my point of view. I kissed her goodnight, turned off the light and settled down to sleep.

* * *

For almost a year, Anita had been aware that her own attitude to Christianity had been undergoing a change. It had begun, rather explosively, several months earlier when she had received the news that the husband of a college friend was dying of cancer. As she read the letter, Anita found anger welling up inside her. How could this happen to Carol, of all people?

At Teacher's Training College, Anita and Carol had been fellow members of the 'Holy Set'. There were six girls in the friendship group. Their nickname derived from the fact that two of them were engaged to theological students and Carol, a tall, serious girl with no boyfriend at that time, was the daughter of a Methodist minister.

Several years after leaving college, Anita had heard with pleasure of Carol's marriage to a teacher of Religious Education, whom she had met whilst working at a comprehensive school in Manchester. Later, news came through the grapevine of the birth of their three children. On two occasions, over the years, Anita and Carol had met, and Anita was pleased to find that her old college chum had blossomed into a happy, capable and loving wife.

Now this! How grossly unfair life was! Anita was upset and deeply hurt at the thought of Carol losing her husband. She was also incensed by the injustice of the situation. She felt an inner fury which would have been heaped upon God – had she but believed in him! She was certainly glad she was now an atheist. How could a *loving* God allow tragedies of this sort to occur in the lives of Christians – his followers? With this sort of God as a *friend*, she reasoned, who needed enemies?

Within a few weeks, Carol became a widow. Anita wrote a letter of sympathy, finding difficulty in expressing her deep sorrow. Carol, in reply, wrote that before his death, she and her husband had prayed that if there was to be no miracle of healing, Carol would be given the strength to overcome her grief. She added that she felt God had supported her, and would continue to do so in the future.

Anita had been disturbed by the intensity of her own feelings, and it was some weeks before she recovered her composure. On one occasion, she found herself recounting the events that had so upset her to Jean Robinson, David's guitar teacher. Jean lived locally and visited our home every Tuesday evening to give David his lesson, and on one such occasion Anita told her the tragic story. Soon they were engaged in a discussion about their respective beliefs and convictions.

Jean was a Christian and a member of the local Methodist Church. She amazed Anita by her simple faith and humble acceptance of events as they happened. Basically, Jean believed God loved her and she trusted him completely. He would take care of her and had her best interests at heart. All she needed to do was follow him. Anita felt rather superior. If only it were that simple! Nevertheless, in spite of Jean's unsophisticated arguments, Anita found herself resuming the conversation the following Tuesday and before many weeks had passed, a regular discussion over a cup of tea had become a feature of their times together.

The relationship had little time to develop however, for within a few months Jean and her family moved out of the district and the discussions came to an end.

They were to recommence unexpectedly and much sooner than could have been anticipated, for as Jean moved out of Anita's life, a hairdresser moved in!

Chapter Seventeen

A Change of Direction

Soon after Jean Robinson left, Anita booked her first appointment with a hair stylist, Peter Wilson, to whom she had been recommended by a friend. Bookings were made by telephone and clients were visited in their own homes.

The day came. Peter arrived. Anita found herself opening the front door to a bearded man in his late twenties, dressed in a T-shirt and jeans and carrying a black holdall.

She watched with interest as he set up a mirror in the kitchen, but felt apprehensive as she sat in front of it. It had taken years for her hair to grow to its present length – almost to her waist – and now she had decided to have it cut into a short style. Peter insisted that he should have total control over the operation, so Anita tried to relax and began to make polite conversation.

She found out that Peter was soon to visit his sister who lived in the south of England and was married to a Pentecostal minister. Peter said he admired her faith and lifestyle, but confessed that her way of life was much too difficult for him. He intended to do things in his own way – and there was no place in it for Christianity.

Anita agreed with him. She said that, like Peter, she had a certain admiration for those who had a faith to guide them, but was unwilling to be restricted by any set of beliefs whatsoever. Once bitten, twice shy.

During the following months, at each successive appointment, Anita saw major changes taking place in Peter's life. By the time he made his next visit he had been to stay with his sister and decided to go to church occasionally. Five weeks later, he told her he had committed his life to Christ! And then, on each subsequent visit, an unexpected change occurred in Peter's lifestyle.

Firstly, he stopped smoking! He didn't find it easy, but eventually he succeeded.

Secondly, he increased his prices! Since becoming a self-employed, free-lance hair stylist, Peter had done his share of tax-fiddling. On his next visit to style Anita's hair he told her that as he was now completing his income tax return honestly, he would have to charge more!

The third and most traumatic change that Anita witnessed concerned Peter's personal life. For two years, he had been living with his girlfriend. But since becoming a Christian, Peter felt challenged by the whole situation. He felt they should no longer live together as man and wife without having made to each other the deep and lasting commitment that is embodied in a marriage ceremony. Unsettled by this, Peter's girlfriend decided to move to London. He was saddened that she was leaving and still felt a strong responsibility towards her, but as a new Christian he knew he could not continue in a relationship that was not based on Christian principles.

Gradually, Peter's life became more settled, but Anita realised that he had become a different person. During his monthly visits, long after the hair styling had been completed, he and Anita would find themselves deep in conversation. Peter would talk about changes in his life that had occurred in the previous weeks, and was full of enthusiasm for his new faith and lifestyle.

Despite her determined resistance, Anita could not suppress a reawakening of her interest in Christianity. Slowly but surely her hard atheistic attitude to life had begun to soften.

* * *

When the Christmas holidays of 1976 arrived, Anita and I were as tired, and relieved, as usual. The lead up to Christmas in primary schools is hectic and exhausting and this year had been no exception. Christmas trees had been erected and decorated; streamers had been festooned around classrooms; carol services and concerts had been arranged; parties for pupils had been organised; and now with everything completed and all decorations taken down and stored away again, we had broken up for the holiday. And it was still three days from Christmas!

When the time came for our own celebrations at home, feelings of apathy and melancholy came over us. Christmas Eve found us trying to stir up enough enthusiasm to play Monopoly with David and Lisa. The children were excited at the prospect of receiving their presents, but I was bored, and my boredom gradually transmitted itself to Anita. That night we went to bed under a grey cloud of unaccountable gloom.

Early on Christmas morning, as Anita made the bed, a wave of disappointment swept over her.

"I'm fed up!" she said to herself, for no one else was in the room. "This is the last Christmas I shall be an atheist!"

Partly surprised by the strength of her own feelings and amused by the determination in her own pronouncement, she laughed out loud.

At the time, I knew nothing about this incident. My inner feelings of boredom persisted. Christmas Day and Boxing Day were spent in being the 'jovial host' as we entertained elderly relatives in our home. Thankfully for me, the two days passed quickly and smoothly and almost before we realised it Christmas was over for another year.

In retrospect, I realise that Anita's declaration to the bedclothes marked the beginning of a spiritual reawakening. Having talked with Jean Robinson and witnessed Peter Wilson's conversion to Christianity, she had become aware that an important element was missing from her life.

When, three days later, Anita and I revealed to each other for the first time our mutual contemplation of God, neither of us knew that we had reached a similar stage in our spiritual development. Each of us had been spiritually activated, but as yet had no outlet for the condition. Just as a radio set may be switched on but remain ineffective until tuned to a particular frequency, we too were aware that a stimulating power had been released into us, but were unable to transform the power into action or purposeful thought.

It took some time for me to make any further progress. I continued to read "Good News for Modern Man" every night and remained in a state of spiritual suspension for weeks. Not so with Anita. Within a few days she had begun to move forward again.

* * *

The days following Christmas were clear and crisp, and a sprinkling of snow added new interest to familiar surroundings. We decided to take advantage of the bright mornings and invigorating fresh air so each day, wrapped in coats and scarves, we set off for a brisk walk around the neighbourhood. The streets of Rochdale are not renowned for their great beauty, but in contrast to the dull routine of necessary car journeys, we found the morning walks along less familiar pathways exhilarating and refreshing.

In addition to our expeditions, I had decided to take up my old hobby of watercolour painting. I had re-discovered an old paint box hidden away at the back of a drawer and had embarked on a series of snow scenes with some enthusiasm. It was a relief to find that the boredom and discontentment I had felt over the Christmas period was disappearing.

On the Sunday following Christmas, Anita and I returned from our walk with scarlet noses and tingling fingers. After a hot drink, I went up to our bedroom to do some further work on my latest masterpiece, and Anita got out the ironing board in the kitchen and switched on the radio for company.

The 'Morning Service' was just drawing to a close. The Bishop of Edmonton was concluding a talk on the roles of various family members in a Christian household. Anita enjoyed what he said but her attention was caught when he announced that his subject on the following Sunday would be 'Making a New Start with God'. He said it was especially aimed at those Christians who had become disillusioned, demoralised or merely lazy. As a folk group concluded the programme with a song, Anita resolved to listen to the service on the following Sunday.

1. The Holy Set – Anita's
College Friendship Group.
Anita is second from the left.

2. Rod and Friend Sunbathing in
Jacket and Long Trousers

3. Bride and Bridesmaids

4. The Bride

5. Cutting the Cake

6. Married at last!

7. One day Honeymoon

8. Our children, David and Lisa

9. Marriage Encounter Team 1989

10. Fifty-fifth Wedding Anniversary with Bridesmaids

11. Senior citizens

Chapter Eighteen

Action!

The next seven days passed quickly. Anita listened to the service on the radio as planned and decided to attend the evening service at our local Methodist Church. However, during his sermon, the local preacher had related long, dull anecdotes which Anita had found bewildering. They seemed to bear no relation to the God *she* was seeking.

Walking home afterwards, Anita reflected on the events of the day. It seemed ages since the morning service on the radio led by the Bishop of Edmonton. His theme had tied in well with the first Sunday of the New Year.

His talk had been full of practical suggestions for 'beginning again with God'. To lapsed churchgoers he had recommended giving church a try. To those who were tired of a particular form of service he suggested attending a different church. He had emphasised the need for a time of quietness or prayer every day, and had advised those in need of help to seek out a fellow Christian or friend in whom they could confide.

However, that night as she went to bed, Anita was aware that her 'new beginning with God' had not really got off the ground. Something more was needed. What on earth should she do?

The answer came into her mind as she lay in bed. Many months ago she had heard Jean Robinson speak of the Minister at Champness Hall – the Central Methodist Hall in Rochdale. Jean had been his secretary before leaving the district. Anita decided to visit him on the following day and ask his advice. With a more settled mind, she went to sleep.

Monday morning dawned. Having seen the family off to school, Anita set off for Champness Hall. With pounding heart, she pushed open the heavy wooden doors, made her way through the foyer, and climbed the wide stone staircase.

The sound of men's voices came from an office on her right. She hesitated outside the door, wondering whether to knock, when suddenly it opened and a middle-aged man appeared. He looked at Anita enquiringly.

"Please can you tell me where I can find the Minister?" she asked.

"I'm the person you are looking for," he replied with a smile. He ushered Anita into an adjoining room, invited her to take a seat, and said he would be back in a moment.

Anita sat down and looked around the room. Why had she come? How could she explain? Her courage began to ebb away. She was considering how she could creep out of the room and slip away unobserved, when the Minister suddenly reappeared and escorted her into his study.

"Well now," he said, "What can I do for you?"

After a hesitant beginning, Anita found the story came pouring out of her. She introduced herself and gave a brief resumé of her life. She had been very religious when young, but everything had gone wrong and eventually she had had a breakdown. As a result she had become an atheist, but recently there had been a sort of reawakening. She was aware of God again. She wanted to pray – but to whom? She had visited a church and found it boring. Could he give her some advice?

As she finished, Anita looked across the desk expectantly but the Minister, John Jennings, reacted in an unexpected way.

He said, "I think I'll ask my wife to see you. You have much in common with her. You have some shared experiences..."

He picked up his telephone and made arrangements for Anita to meet his wife in the manse at 8.30 p.m. that evening.

* * *

Lynne Jennings gave Anita a warm welcome. She was ushered into the lounge, and within a few minutes the two women were deep in conversation.

Anita found Lynne easy to talk to, and it was great to converse with a Christian who seemed to be on her wavelength. Lynne gave examples of various acquaintances who had been converted to Christianity after years of apathy or atheism. Anita listened to what she said but expressed her own doubts and fears. Truth to tell, she had heard it all before. What it came down to in the end was belief. Either one did or did not believe. It was as simple as that.

Suddenly however, her attention was caught by a story Lynne had begun to tell about the healing of a woman with rheumatoid arthritis. Lynne described how, during a service at which she was speaking, she had noticed a woman so severely crippled with arthritis that she could not walk without the aid of sticks. At the end of the service, Lynne asked the woman if she would like to be prayed with. The woman agreed. Prayers were said, and the congregation was amazed to see the woman raise her arms in worship, and later she was able to move about freely without her sticks. The improvement in her condition was dramatic and seemed permanent – she left the church some time later unaided and overjoyed.

However, Lynne's feelings of elation at the healing had been quickly deflated. She learned that her prayers for healing had met with the disapproval of several senior church members. They made it clear that they did not want 'this sort of thing' to be repeated in future.

As Anita listened to the story, she was aware of her own physical condition. She had been suffering from rheumatoid arthritis for several years and still attended the Rheumatism Clinic at Manchester Royal Infirmary where the illness had been brought under control. For three years, with the help of a number of drugs, she had been almost back to normal. Although she knew she was unlikely to recover from the illness, she was thankful that she could lead a relatively normal life.

The story of the healing of the arthritic woman made a strong impression on Anita. In the discussion that followed, Lynne expressed her view that arthritis sometimes appeared to manifest physically an inner bitterness which was distorting the personality of the sufferer.

Their conversation continued. Two hours flew by and the time came for Anita to leave. As she waved goodbye to Lynne and drove homewards, she was glad she had made the visit. She felt that she had taken a positive step in her search for God.

Chapter Nineteen

A Miracle?

Anita's positive steps contrasted sharply with my lack of spiritual activity. I found her impulsive decisions to go to church and visit a minister at his home somewhat bewildering, and I had no desire to emulate her actions!

In retrospect, I seemed to live through the early weeks of 1977 in a state of frustrated agitation. The responsibilities of my new job as head teacher of an open-plan primary school were weighing heavily upon me. The winter was relatively mild and the flu germs were having a field day. Staff absences were causing considerable difficulties, and almost daily I found myself having to teach a class of children and carry out my Head's duties simultaneously. Most evenings were spent recovering from exhaustion!

But towards the end of January, it began to dawn on me that there was something different about Anita. Over a period of days, the thought that something was odd had crept imperceptibly into my subconscious brain. It was a sort of hazy notion that skipped around just inside my mind, but just outside my comprehension. I couldn't detect anything in her behaviour to justify its existence – yet it wouldn't go away.

One evening, the penny dropped. Over the last few years I had become accustomed to seeing Anita's movements restricted by rheumatoid arthritis. When she got up from a chair, there would be a brief pause as she straightened her legs; when holding a pan, her two-handed grip indicated her weak wrists; her hold on a door handle was loose and ineffective. As we relaxed in front of the television one evening, I suddenly realised that the change I had been unable to detect in Anita was the *absence* of the stiffness and weakness I had grown used to. As she moved about, there were no little pauses, no slightly bent knees, no twinges of pain, no requests for help. I was puzzled.

"How's the arthritis nowadays? Is it getting any better?"

Anita looked up from her sewing.

"It's almost gone," she replied, "and I haven't taken any tablets for over a week!"

I stared at her with raised eyebrows.

"What do you mean?" I asked incredulously.

Anita began to explain. On the evening of her return from Lynne and John Jennings' home, she had been unable to sleep. Her mind was in a whirl. Her thoughts kept wandering back over the events of the day: her visit to Champness Hall; the interview with John Jennings; her conversation with Lynne. Eventually, afraid that her tossing and turning would awaken me, she decided to go downstairs and make a cup of tea.

Sitting in the lounge, sipping her tea, she found herself wondering if her arthritis could be caused by bitterness. Lynne had suggested there might be a connection, and the psychotherapy sessions years ago had revealed feelings of resentment which went way back to her childhood. Suddenly, Anita's wandering thoughts focused on God and she spoke aloud:

"I don't know if you're there God, and I don't even know if I believe in you. But if you *are* there, it would be a really good idea for you to cure my arthritis. If it's caused by bitterness or resentment, God, just root it out of me. I'm not saying I'll never believe in you if my arthritis *isn't* cured, but it would be a jolly good way of proving your existence. And if you *do* take it away, I'll never doubt you again."

Then she finished her tea, returned to bed, and fell fast asleep.

When Anita opened her eyes next morning, memories of her prayer flooded back into her mind. Carefully, and hopefully, she moved her arms and legs around to see how they felt. They felt very much the same as usual. There was no improvement. As she got out of bed and experienced the familiar ache and stiffness in her joints, she knew there had been no miracle cure.

"Ah well," she sighed, "Nothing's been lost if nothing gained."

A miraculous overnight healing would have been too good to be true, she reasoned. Nevertheless, that day Anita decided not to take her tablets, and by evening felt no worse. Gradually over the next few days the effects of the arthritis faded. She found her grip gradually strengthening and full mobility returning to her wrists. She was able to get out of bed in the morning and straighten her legs immediately as she began to dress. She could manipulate the blankets and tuck in the sheets as she made the beds. Her swollen joints began to resume normal proportions. Within a week her symptoms had all but disappeared. The dull background ache to which she had grown so accustomed faded away.

As Anita related the story to me, I could scarcely believe it. I made her repeat the essential facts again, trying to find a logical explanation for what had happened. It was impossible.

"Look at my wrists," she said, bending each one back to an angle of ninety degrees. I just looked at her, bewildered. Months previously, she had been given a pair of flesh-coloured splints at the Rheumatism Clinic. They were pink cylindrical tubes which were designed to fit around each forearm with the aid of velcro strips. Their purpose was to hold her wrists and hands straight, in direct line with her arms. The doctors were concerned that Anita's hands were becoming restricted to an inward curving position, increasing her disability. Now, she was waggling her wrists around with ease, and looking at me with a mixture of happiness and wonder on her face.

My attempts to work out for myself how the cure had come about were frustrating and fruitless – but I kept on trying! The fact that I couldn't think of a satisfactory explanation was a source of worry and annoyance. For days, my mind dwelt on such words as 'autosuggestion' and 'psychosomatic'. I rehearsed the arguments to myself.

Argument One: Perhaps the talk about arthritis with Lynne Jennings had caused some sort of autosuggestion to take place in Anita's brain, thus enabling her to cure herself of arthritis. Was that possible? It didn't sound too convincing!

Argument Two: Maybe the explanation was that Anita's illness had been brought on by her father's death three years earlier. Now – for some reason – she had quite coincidentally recovered.

My theories sounded weak and unconvincing, but I was determined to accept one of them as true! They seemed infinitely preferable to the one that kept haunting me, and for which I could offer no explanation at all. That God had heard Anita's prayer and had somehow lifted the illness from her.

Chapter Twenty

Confusion or Confirmation?

As the days passed and Anita's symptoms did not return, I found myself trying to avoid the conclusion that God had taken the illness from her. As the wheels of a cart follow the ruts in a farm track, so my thoughts about Anita's recovery followed the direction of the set ideas that had developed in me over the years. I preferred to consider the 'cure' as a remission of illness, or put it down to some natural cause that I could explain to myself and to others. To consider it an 'answer to prayer' seemed like coming across a boulder in the cart track. I could not ride over it, yet avoiding it would take me away from the old familiar route and set me on a new course across fields of discovery.

I felt unsettled emotionally. Thankful, yet uncomfortable. What answer should I give when relatives or friends asked after Anita's health? To reply that all signs of her arthritis had disappeared would provoke further questions. And I wondered how people would react if I answered casually:

"Thanks for asking. She's cured. God's worked a miracle on her, you know!"

The idea of saying such a thing filled me with alarm.

My anxiety centred around the fear of being regarded as a religious crank. I thought of the elderly men who parade the streets in city centres with placards encouraging us to 'REPENT, THE END OF THE WORLD IS NIGH' or serious-faced students who enquire earnestly if one is 'saved'. To accept that God was real and active seemed to put me in the same bracket as people whom I thought were neurotic!

Here was I, master of most situations, with a well-ordered existence, a comfortable home and a happy family. How could I cope with a God who intervened unexpectedly and required worshipping?

* * *

Weeks passed. Anita remained healthy and I remained confused. Anita's next appointment at the Rheumatism Clinic in Manchester was booked for 15th March. On each of these three-monthly visits she had to provide samples of urine and blood for testing, and undergo a rigorous physical examination by a doctor. Often she returned from the hospital in some pain resulting from the squeezing of her hands and wrists, and the manipulation of other joints. These appointments were to assess Anita's physical condition and to determine whether the prescribed dose of her tablets was effectively controlling the disease. Over the last two years it had remained constant at three tablets a day, but for the last five weeks she had taken no tablets at all!

The day of the appointment dawned. I left for work that morning wondering what the outcome of Anita's visit would be. I was keen to hear a medical opinion on her recovery. Whilst confirmation of a cure would fill us both with joy, it would undoubtedly cause me much heart-searching.

"What happened?" I asked as I hurried in through the doorway, not even pausing to put down my briefcase. "What did the doctor say?"

"There's not a sign of active rheumatoid arthritis in my body," replied Anita, then added with a laugh, "The doctor says I can stop taking my tablets now!"

She told me how, on arrival at hospital, she had gone through the usual routine of providing specimens, and then undressed in a cubicle. The specialist had arrived and begun his examination.

"How are you today?" he had asked after reading Anita's notes, and had begun to manipulate her wrists and press the bones in her hands. She had told him she felt very well.

As he finished his examination, he had said, "You're a fraud coming here today. There's no sign of arthritis in your joints. You can stop taking the chloroquine phosphate now – and just take the naproxen if you stiffen up." Turning to leave, he added, "We'll see how you go on until your next appointment. If the tests are clear next time we may be able to discharge you."

Neither of us knew then that six months later she *would* be discharged, and that the specimens she had given that day *would* show the disease had become inactive. Such additional proof was not available and not necessary. For both of us, the visit had been confirmation of Anita's recovery.

* * *

It was at this point that I abandoned my three-month-old resolution not to discuss religion with Anita. How could one *not* discuss such a series of remarkable events as those we had witnessed in the last few weeks? Anita was well and happy, and I was overjoyed to see her healthy again. We spoke at length about all that had happened. Anita had no doubts about the reason for her recovery. She had asked God to remove the illness, and had given a pledge that were he to do so, she would believe in his existence. With her return to health came an inner certainty that God had healed her.

In contrast to Anita, I still felt unsure of myself. I was uncertain how to view her recovery, uncertain about God, uncertain what to do. I kept going over the facts of the case, hoping to discern in them some 'magical' quality that would point incontrovertibly to God's supernatural intervention. It took many days for me to realise that the real problem that faced me was one of interpretation, not comprehension. It was obvious really. Like those football matches I used to watch.

Years earlier, I had been a regular supporter of Rochdale Association Football Club. When the team were playing at home I could be found on the terraces at Spotland, cheering on the players to greater efforts. I always stood in exactly the same place on the football ground. That's where I used to meet George and his mate. I knew George as our local road sweeper – he used to drop in occasionally for a cup of tea. I never found out what his friend was called but he was an avid Rochdale supporter.

Each Saturday, he saw an entirely different game from George and me. He saw pushes in the back by members of the opposing team which George and I somehow missed; he saw deliberate fouls on our players which we did not notice; and he was certain of 'offside' on almost every occasion that our opponents scored. It was amazing at times to realise that we were all watching the same match, because we interpreted the same events so differently.

My problem now was how to interpret Anita's recovery – as an act of God, or otherwise.

Eventually comprehension began to dawn on me amidst the mists of confusion. The events that had occurred were *facts*. One could describe them in a modern way using medical jargon – "remission" – or in a spiritual way – "healing". The terminology did not affect the reality. Anita's return to health was an occasion for joy and thankfulness whether it was described as a remission of illness or a miracle of healing.

I began to realise that both descriptions were valid. I had justified my preference for the modern, scientific description of Anita's recovery as a more logical, rational assessment of the event, but now it dawned on me that I could no more explain to myself the meaning of "remission of illness" than "act of healing". Whilst I was not prepared to believe that the cure was a gift from God, I was willing to accept it as a coincidental occurrence. I knew too that I was experiencing feelings of thankfulness which were being frustrated – for it is not possible to be truly grateful for a happy accident.

The nub of my problem was that I had not the faith to believe in a loving, caring God, even though there was strong evidence that seemed to point to his existence.

Chapter Twenty-one

Back to York

One evening late in March, as Anita and I were about to switch off the T.V., our attention was caught by an item on the nightly current affairs programme. It was a filmed report about a church in York that was experimenting with new forms of worship, including drama and dance. Surprisingly, in contrast to the current trend, it was filled to capacity every Sunday.

Our interest aroused, Anita and I decided to stay up to watch it. The film was about St. Michael le Belfry, a church close to York Minster. Opening shots of the city and the surrounding countryside reawakened in us memories of the holiday we had so much enjoyed. However, within minutes the programme had settled into its central theme. Film was shown of the interior of St. Michael's, and a background commentary began to describe how a new wave of vitality and enthusiasm was present in the services.

Anita and I watched with interest as extracts from a service were shown. In front of the altar was a large square carpeted dais. On this platform, at intervals, various groups of people actively participated in the service. On one occasion a group of musicians with guitars and other instruments accompanied their own singing, and that of the whole congregation. At another time, some young women and children translated their praise into movement and dance. Forming a circle, they crossed and re-crossed, gliding and leaping gracefully, arms high in the air, their actions capturing the joy of the song the congregation was singing. In another shot, the drama group was shown illustrating bible readings, their portrayal adding a new emphasis to some well-known passage of scripture. In closing, the commentator spoke of the many groups of Christians in Britain who were beginning to spread the gospel in unconventional ways. In the face of controversy about their methods, they pointed to evidence that many churches, once assumed dead, were undergoing a process of renewal.

As I switched off the T.V. set, I realised that it was a group of people from this same St. Michael's Church who had performed the sketches many months earlier in the courtyard off Stonegate. Since that evening so much had happened to us. My life had undergone a change and now, in a strange way I seemed to have come full circle. I thought it was time for another visit to York.

When, soon afterwards, Anita suggested an Easter break in the caravan, I knew instinctively what was in her mind. I completed the booking form and sent it off to the Caravan Club reserving a place on the site next to Rowntree Park.

We decided to travel there on Maundy Thursday and to return home the following Wednesday. The site was ideal for a spring holiday, we reasoned. There were plenty of interesting buildings to visit if the weather was wet and we would be within easy walking distance of the city centre. We hardly mentioned to each other our intention of attending the Easter services at St. Michael's, but it was clearly in both our minds. Anita had been attracted by the vitality and commitment that had come over so strongly in the T.V. programme. My interest lay in the hope that such a visit might help to resolve my never-ending difficulty with 'faith'. And so our differing motives blended into a single, unspoken ambition.

* * *

It was at about this time that it slowly began to dawn on me that the final step in becoming a Christian would involve me in a sort of spiritual parachute jump. The thought filled me with apprehension. I would have much preferred a series of logical stepping stones which ended in positive proof of God's existence – at which point I would have committed myself to his service! But now I began to realise that this was not to be. If I were to become a Christian I had to jump!

A paratrooper, waiting in the aeroplane, needs to have an inner certainty that his parachute will open. His ability to step out into space hinges on his conviction that he will be safe and supported. And yet, until he has made the leap, and felt the pull on his shoulders and seen the billowing silk umbrella above him, he has no proof that his confidence is justified.

Metaphorically speaking, I was teetering on the edge of the jumping platform. The new spirituality within me and the previous months' experiences had given me increasing confidence that God was alive, active and caring. But I found the single step forward that would launch me from the secure platform of knowledge to the unpredictability of faith impossible to take.

In trying to rationalise my fears, I kept questioning God's reason for requiring such a step. Why did he choose such an incomprehensible way of being discovered? I asked myself. It didn't make sense! The answer came unexpectedly one evening as I was reading 'Good News for Modern Man'. In following the reading plan, I had arrived at Paul's first letter to the Corinthians. As I read the first chapter, the words suddenly leapt from the page, startling me by the direct way in which they answered the question that was troubling me.

"For God in His wisdom made it impossible for people to know him by means of their own wisdom. Instead, by means of the so-called 'foolish' message we preach, God decided to save those who believe."

I had often wondered how God 'spoke' to people and how he 'answered' prayer. As a teenager, I had sometimes heard my parents talking about someone who had been 'called' into the ministry, or even to the mission field. The whole business was completely beyond the realm of my experience. As I grew older, if I thought about such matters at all, my view was that the person concerned was either neurotic, or was attributing to God a desire which came from his own subconscious.

Now, as I read this chapter from Paul's letter to the people of Corinth, questions regarding the audibility of the divine voice became purely academic. A sudden shaft of insight struck to the very centre of my understanding, and the conundrum became instantly comprehensible. The step of faith was God's method of providing *equal opportunity* of access to himself. A method that was not dependent on education, social class, age, colour, sex – even nationality! The reason I could never get to God by a series of logical steps was because that method of access would preclude millions of people – the uneducated, the mentally handicapped, the very young, the illogical!

I read on, mentally reeling under the impact of the new perspective suddenly revealed.

"...For what seems to be God's foolishness is wiser than human wisdom, and what seems to be God's weakness is stronger than human strength..."

"...God has made Christ to be our wisdom. By him we are put right with God; we become God's holy people and are set free."

At last, I really began to understand what was required. Faith in Jesus Christ was the way to God, and every one, no matter how young or old, simple or sophisticated, serious or carefree had equal access, because all groups were capable of believing.

* * *

A fortnight later, as we set off for our Easter holiday, an idea that had been gradually forming in my mind crystallised into a resolution. At some time over the Easter weekend, I was going to take the final step and become a Christian. It seemed appropriate that this should happen in York, and as I already felt a link with St. Michael's Church, I hoped to forge my agreement with God during one of the services there.

Looking back now, I am amazed at my arrogance and spiritual naivety. The truth is that my concept of Christianity was riddled with misunderstandings. I looked upon becoming a Christian as reaching the end of the road – a once-for-all action, complete in itself. I had no expectations of any developments taking place following my step of faith, and did not see it in any way as making a new start, or beginning a new lifestyle. In addition, I definitely expected an unmistakable sign of God's acceptance of me in recognition of my belief in his existence. I stipulated that it must be remarkable and recognisable – but I would accept his choice of what it would be!

We drew on to the Caravan Club Site in York at lunchtime on Maundy Thursday. In less than an hour we had levelled the caravan, set up the water containers, brewed a pot of tea, and were looking forward to our first holiday of 1977.

Chapter Twenty-two

The Parachute Jump

As Anita and I left the caravan to attend the service at St. Michael's on Good Friday morning, we made one last attempt to persuade David to come with us. Lisa was happy to accompany us, but David was determined to stay at home.

"The service will be very interesting," coaxed Anita. "There may be actors or people dancing. It should be good."

Her encouraging words fell on deaf ears.

"Will they talk about Jesus?"

"Well, yes," I replied hesitantly, "I suppose they will."

"Then I don't want to come," said David. "It's not my thing."

I had no right to expect David to show a sudden enthusiasm for attending a church service. In the past I had certainly not encouraged him to take an interest in religion.

When the children were young, Anita and I had strongly resisted our parents' attempts to persuade us to have them christened.

No, we had said - it would be hypocritical of us to go through some form of dedication service when we had no intention of honouring our vows.

Did we not think we should have it done for the children's sake? we were asked.

No, we had said, we did not. Our children would have plenty of time to decide whether they believed in God when they grew up – there was no need to make promises on their behalf during infancy.

Subdued by our determination if not by our logical arguments, our parents eventually gave in. The children were not christened, nor given any Christian teaching at home.

When David was seven, he asked if he could go to Sunday school. Our neighbour's two children, with whom he was friendly, had mentioned they were regular attenders and had invited him along. He went off happily with them one Sunday morning, accompanied by Lisa.

Remembering our own Sunday school days, Anita and I looked at each other with raised eyebrows as David and friends, waving cheerfully, turned the corner and disappeared from sight.

"I bet that doesn't last long," I said with a smile.

However, neither of us expected his interest to wane quite as quickly as it did. When he returned home two hours later, David looked crestfallen.

"Did you enjoy it?" I had asked. "What happened?"

"It was boring," he had said, shrugging his shoulders. "All we did was talk about Jesus."

"That's what Sunday school is for," I replied knowingly.

"Well, it's not my thing," said David – and he never went to Sunday school again.

* * *

Anita, Lisa and I reached the Church of St. Michael le Belfrey at ten past ten on Good Friday morning. Although the service did not begin until ten thirty, several families were already entering by a side door. After a moment's pause we followed them in.

We found ourselves in an entrance hall, partitioned from the worship area by an oak and glass screen. Several people were standing around perusing books, colourful leaflets and other items of interest that were on display. We passed through to the worship area, selected a side pew and sat down a little self-consciously.

As I looked around I saw that the interior of the church was light and spacious. The walls were painted white. Two rows of slender stone pillars, running from front to back, supported the gently curving arches of the roof. There was a gallery across the back of the church and to my right, in the chancel, was the raised carpeted dais remembered from the television programme. Hanging from the pillars were banners depicting Christ's death on the cross and, in keeping with the theme of Good Friday, three large wooden crosses stood on the dais.

The church was already half filled by people. There were family groups comprising parents and children of all ages; many young couples in their early twenties; university students; elderly men and women who had come alone, and several people easily identified as visitors to York by their cagoules and heavy walking shoes.

The interior of the church buzzed with quiet conversation. People smiled. Family groups and individuals greeted each other warmly with words, handshakes and embraces. Here and there hands were waved in recognition of friends across the room. Children chattered and babes in arms gurgled, fingering their mothers' faces. The atmosphere was one of warmth and hospitality.

By half past ten every seat was filled. Extra chairs were placed in the aisles to accommodate late-comers. A congregation of several hundred people waited for the service to begin. I had been so preoccupied in watching the people enter, and impressed by their happy, friendly faces that the main reason for my visit had slipped from my mind. Now, in the quiet moments before the service, my resolution returned. I bowed my head in prayer.

"This is it, God," I murmured. "I want to take the step of faith that I've been holding back from. Just help me do it!"

I cannot remember the order of the service in detail. I was aware that everyone was participating fully, and that people of all ages were deeply involved in worship. There was a reality about the happenings that contrasted sharply with all my previous experiences of church services. The building was full of joy. The singing was enthusiastic and sincere. The dancing and drama groups' contributions were lively and creative, adding new dimensions to a well-known theme. The sermon was short, clear and visual. The three crosses on the dais were used effectively to illustrate the message of Good Friday. Time passed quickly. Almost before I realised it we were standing to sing the final hymn. The service was drawing to a close.

I wondered when I should voice my personal prayer of commitment. I had waited for a suitable moment – yet one had not arisen. Then, suddenly, an idea came into my mind. If I participated in the communion service, I would be able to make my step of faith during the act of taking bread and wine, and it would be symbolised in a clear, physical way. I liked the idea. I decided then and there that it was the right thing to do.

As the final hymn ended I leaned closer to Anita.

"I'd like to stay for communion after the service," I whispered. "Would you?"

We bowed our heads for the final blessing which brought the service to a close. When we raised them again, I looked at Anita.

"It's Good Friday." she replied. "There isn't a communion service today. The last communion service before Easter is on Maundy Thursday. The next will be on Sunday, Easter Day."

Five minutes later we were walking back towards the caravan site in the early spring sunshine. My mind was in a whirl. Somehow or other, my plans had gone awry. I had still not become a Christian. I felt disappointed – as though I had missed an opportunity. The idea of linking my step of faith with the communion service had seemed such a good one, but my best intentions had come to nothing. There was only one thing I could do – make a second attempt on Easter Sunday morning.

* * *

St Michael's had been full on Good Friday, but it was absolutely packed with people on Easter Day. All the extra chairs that had been put in the aisles were occupied and several people, standing in the entrance hall at the rear, seemed to have settled for worshipping from there.

Anita, Lisa and I had arrived early, but even so we had to be satisfied with a side pew situated half way towards the rear of the church. It was not an ideal place from which to see the leader of the service, or the dancers on the dais --but at least we had a seat!

It was a family centred service, full of variety and interest. Everyone was given a warm welcome by the vicar. Then followed a hymn and a prayer and 'birthday time' for the children – young members of the congregation who were celebrating a birthday that week were given a card and asked to choose a chorus for everyone to sing. This was followed by a christening ceremony for two babies, whose parents carried them to the dais for the dedication and sprinkling with water from a small white font. The address was given by the curate. He told the story of the empty tomb on Easter morning, illustrating his talk with coloured slides projected on to a screen at the front to the church.

As the service ended an announcement was made. Those members of the congregation, irrespective of denomination, who had asked Jesus Christ to be their Saviour were invited to stay for a short communion service which was to follow. One or two parents with very young children began to leave, and Anita, Lisa and I took the opportunity to move to the pew behind us, which became empty. As we stretched our limbs, relieving the cramp resulting from an hour in an overcrowded pew, I began to feel apprehensive. This was my first ever communion and I was not sure how the bread and wine would be administered or what was expected of me as I received it. But I knew I must go through with it. There could be no turning back now.

* * *

It was not until two or three weeks after Easter that I realised my request had been answered. I had asked for an unmistakable and remarkable sign of God's acceptance of me in acknowledgement of my step of faith. Yet when it came, I had failed to recognise it. I think there were two reasons for this. Firstly, I was expecting something 'supernatural' (lightning flashes and thunderclaps at least!). Secondly, at the time the sign was hidden from me by my own anxiety.

As the communion service in the church of St. Michael le Belfry began, my intention to mark my step of faith by taking bread and wine seemed right – yet I was feeling ill at ease. I was finding it difficult to follow the unfamiliar service, and my mind kept focusing on the fact that I didn't know how the bread and wine would be administered. I was also conscious that I was stepping forward into the unknown – the time for my parachute jump had arrived!

At the front of the church several helpers had joined the vicar. There were stewards who were to indicate when members of the congregation should come forward, and clergy and a lay reader who were to help with the administration of the bread and wine. I was glad we were not near the front of the church. Our side pew provided a good vantage point. I could watch what everyone else did and, when my turn came, copy their behaviour.

Prayers were offered for the bread and wine, and then the stewards began to move into place ready to open the pew doors. It was clear that the hundreds of people present were to be ushered forward in an orderly manner. The steward on our side of the church walked up the aisle and stood quite close to where we were sitting. My heart skipped a beat. Surely they would begin at the front of the church – or the back? I watched anxiously as he placed his hand on the pew door at the front of the next row, and looked towards the ministers on the dais.

The nod from the vicar was almost imperceptible, but the steward picked up the signal. Momentarily, his hand began to open the pew door on which it rested. Then, quite purposefully, he made straight for our pew. He opened the door and indicated with a nod that we should go forward for communion.

A wave of panic swept over me as I stepped out into the aisle. I was first! My mouth was dust-dry and my knees were knocking. It seemed unbelievable. Out of a congregation of eleven hundred people, I was first. I had not the faintest idea what to do. Suddenly, my desperation gave rise to inspiration. With a gesture of politeness, I stepped to one side and allowed Anita to walk out to the front before me.

We had joked about it afterwards.

"What a coincidence!" Anita had said.

"Unbelievable," I had replied. "What on earth made them begin at a back pew half way down the side of the Church?"

I had laughed at my temporary embarrassment but missed the point. I had been on the look-out for thunderclaps and lightning flashes, but God's sign was just as amazing. As I had accepted him in faith, he had sealed the act with an unquestionable and memorable experience. On Easter Day 1977, Anita and I were the first two people in a congregation of many hundreds, to receive communion in the Church of St. Michael le Belfry, York.

* * *

The rest of our holiday was spent exploring York and surrounding places of interest with our children and we returned home on the Wednesday after Easter. Within an hour or two I felt as if I had never been away. The children and I had unloaded our equipment from the caravan, and Anita had loaded the washing into the machine. By teatime, everything was back to normal. Inwardly, I felt disappointed. During the three days I had been a Christian nothing different had happened. Nothing whatsoever! My behaviour had been the same as before. I must have had a notion that Christianity would somehow transform me overnight from a caterpillar into a magnificent butterfly. Finding myself still very much at home on my familiar cabbage patch left me feeling disillusioned and disgruntled.

After tea, I settled down to read the local newspaper which is published twice weekly. On our return from York we had found the Wednesday edition lying behind the front door. I began to leaf through the pages in a random manner, catching up on local news as I glanced from item to item. Suddenly, an advertisement caught my eye. It was displayed prominently on the 'public announcements' page.

'Did you see Jesus of Nazareth?' the headline asked.

The question referred to the Robert Powell film that had been screened on television in two parts over the Easter weekend. Although

CHAPTER TWENTY-TWO

I had not seen the programmes, I continued to read the smaller print below.

'If you were moved by the film and would like to meet real people trying to live the Christian life here in Rochdale, write or make a phone call to:

Rev. Mike Wood

West Street Baptist Church

Rochdale'

I was surprised to realise that I did not know where West Street Baptist Church was situated. During the fifteen years I had lived in Rochdale I had gained a good knowledge of most areas of the town, but I had never even heard of West Street.

I re-read the advertisement and found myself wondering whether I should follow it up.

I dismissed the thought immediately. What would be the use of that? I knew nothing of the church or its minister, and I had no reason to believe it was any different from the many other dying churches that advertised their Sunday services in the local newspaper. I tried to curb my impulsiveness and read through the rest of the paper.

Half an hour later found me sitting on the settee, pad on lap, pen poised, wondering what on earth to write. My first attempt was already a screwed up ball of paper. I began again:

Dear Mr. Wood,

I am writing in reply to your advertisement in the 'Rochdale Observer'. No, I did not see 'Jesus of Nazareth' on T.V., but my family and I have just returned from a holiday in York where we attended the Easter services at St. Michael le Belfry.

I feel I have caught a glimpse of what Christianity can be like, and would be pleased if you would send me information or literature about your services at West Street.

Yours sincerely,

P.S. I am nearly forty years of age.

When I showed the letter to Anita, she was amazed.

"Goodness me!" she exclaimed. "It's not like you to reply to advertisements like that." And she was right. It wasn't like me at all.

Chapter Twenty-three

A Visitor

The doorbell rang and I went to answer it. I'd been waiting for this visit for four days, and I felt rather nervous as I opened the front door to the visitor. The light from the hall flooded out to illuminate a tall, bearded figure in his late thirties."Hello," he said. "I'm Mike Wood."

Later, as we sat in our lounge drinking coffee, Anita and I described the ways in which we had felt drawn to God, and how, quite separately, each had taken a step of commitment.

Mike listened with interest and, in return, told us something of his background. His conversion to Christianity had taken place during his teenage years in London. Later, as an insurance broker on course for an interesting and profitable career at Lloyds, he felt that God was calling him to the ministry and entered Spurgeon's College in London to train as a Baptist minister.

For many years, as Pastor of West Street Baptist Church, Mike had used all his ingenuity to try to add to the fourteen or so elderly souls who formed his congregation. All his best efforts seemed to come to nothing. If anything, the group was dwindling year by year as older members died. However, during a serious illness four years previously, Mike had felt that God was telling him to change his ministry. He must preach the gospel, stop trying to organise a revival, and allow God to take the initiative. Quite remarkably, since that time seventy people had joined the church, and many had been baptised by total immersion in water.

Anita and I were fascinated by his story and asked Mike many questions. Within a short time we were conversing with the familiarity of old friends. During the course of that evening, I began to realise that my conversion to Christianity was not a once-for-all experience, but the beginning of a journey. Aglow with enthusiasm, I thought I knew most, if not all, of the answers. However, as time went by and the conversation deepened, it became apparent from Mike's words that true Christianity did not merely touch the surface of one's life, but had far-reaching effects into one's whole lifestyle. The step of commitment Anita and I had taken was likely to result in a whole new experience of life. A fresh start. A second chance. Jesus himself had spoken of "being born again" and I was suddenly conscious that here we were, right at the beginning of a new life. The thought was both exciting and frightening – and much more than I had bargained for!

Mike set off for home well after midnight. We shook hands at the door, and waved goodbye as his car drove off into the distance. It was hard to believe that we had met Mike Wood for the first time that evening. There was a closeness between us that was difficult to understand. It was our first experience of true Christian fellowship.

* * *

Anita and I decided to attend the service at West Street Baptist Church on the following Sunday morning. A few days earlier I had discovered where it was situated and I must admit it came as a shock!

I had been driving along the Rochdale inner ring road one afternoon, when my attention had been caught by a small, blue-edged sign fixed to a lamppost. It pointed to a minor road on my right. The words stood out clearly on the white background, and I took them in at a glance as I drove along.

"West Street Baptist Church"

In the one long second it took the car to pass the end of West Street, my eyes travelled several times up and down its length. I was appalled at what I saw: litter strewn pavements, several neglected and boarded- up properties, and a group of urchins playing in the middle of the road.

"Oh, Glory!" I groaned to the steering wheel.

Five seconds later, I was laughing at my response. Even in my dashed expectations there seemed to be humour – and God's presence. The words I had uttered were totally unexpected – even by me! I had never before used this expression, and the words themselves, voiced in dismay, seemed to express the very opposite of my dejected feelings.

In that moment of laughter, I knew everything was going to be alright. Despite its unpromising surroundings, I felt sure that West Street Baptist Church was the church God had chosen for me.

* * *

David and Lisa were away spending the weekend with Anita's mother in Manchester, so we made our first visit to 'West Street' alone. I parked the car in a convenient position, but having reached what we both took to be the main entrance of the Baptist Church, we discovered that the building had been sold to a commercial firm and was no longer a place of worship. The once stately frontage with its stone pillars and wide flight of stone steps was now painted pink and pale green and covered in graffiti. Somewhat baffled we looked around and saw a narrow, cobbled street which ran alongside the church building.

The line of cars parked along its length and the movement of people through a doorway over a hundred yards away, attracted our attention.

The old Sunday school building was situated behind the former church and as Anita and I approached the entrance, we realised we had reached our destination. The open door led into a well-kept entrance hall. The young man who stood there to welcome us greeted Anita with unexpected enthusiasm.

"Hi there!" he said, shaking her hand vigorously. "How nice to see you. How's David?"

His words took us both by surprise, and I was still intrigued as we entered the schoolroom that was now serving as the worship centre.

"Who was that?" I asked at the first convenient opportunity.

"It's Phil Barratt, David's old guitar teacher – I just didn't expect to see him here."

Months earlier, after Jean Robinson had moved house, we had searched for a guitar teacher to take her place. We had seen an advertisement in the local newspaper and were pleased when Phil Barratt had agreed to take David as a pupil. He was an accomplished guitarist and was young, friendly and reliable. David took to him immediately, and actually enjoyed his daily practice, looking forward to his weekly tutorial at Phil's flat, ferried there by Anita.

Imagine our disappointment when after less than two months, Phil phoned us to say that he was unable to take pupils any longer. His neighbours in the adjoining flats had complained about the noise and disturbance.

David had been so disappointed that we had tried to persuade Phil to continue the lessons in our home, but he had felt unable to do so. He had no car, and his spare time was spent in trying to establish a professional music group. So reluctantly, we had had to accept his decision.

Our meeting with Phil Barratt on that first Sunday morning at 'West Street' was providential – as we discovered later in the day. We picked up the children that afternoon and exchanged news as we drove home. They were delighted that 'Nan' had allowed them to stay up late on the previous evening and had a bottomless store of sweets and crisps.

When David asked how we had spent *our* day I didn't know what to say. I felt unable to describe our visit to church. How could I communicate the warmth of the welcome we had received; the happy, friendly faces of the congregation; the vitality in the worship, and the atmosphere of love within the building which was so reminiscent of that which we had experienced at St. Michael's, York.

Anita stepped in.

"We went to West Street Baptist Church," she said, "and who do you think we saw there? Phil Barratt!"

David looked up.

"What was *he* doing there?"

Anita told how Phil had greeted us at the door and had later played his guitar as a group sang choruses.

David was quiet for a few moments.

CHAPTER TWENTY-THREE

"Will you be going to church next week?" he asked.

We nodded.

"I think I'll come with you," he said.

Chapter Twenty-five

Commitment.

The arrival of my fortieth birthday on 6th August 1977 signalled my entry into that period of life popularly known as middle age. I received the usual cards and good wishes from relatives and friends. Those who knew my date of birth and had worked out how old I was, encouraged me with phrases such as 'Life begins at forty!' For once this cliché was true. I had 'begun again' in the preceding months.

Our children had settled quickly and happily at 'West Street'. From the outset, we had made a conscious decision not to influence their attitude to the church. We were prepared to accept whatever level of involvement each child wanted to give. From their very first visit, the children responded to the friendship so evident amongst the church members. David was attracted by the guitar players and 'Psalm', the singing group, and Lisa quickly made friends with several girls who were her own age. Both children were 'at home' immediately.

Within a week or two, our family of four had been absorbed into the much larger family of 'West Street'. Merely to describe this assimilation as 'joining the church' or 'attending the services regularly' would not reflect accurately the integration that took place. The truth is we were bowled over by the friendship, care and concern which were apparent in the actions of all the church members. People displayed a directness in speech, an honesty in opinion, a generosity in action and a confidence in approach to life that we found breath-taking.

But it was not only their sincerity that made a strong impression on us. Within the church there seemed to exist a framework of deep relationships which crossed barriers of age, sex and class, and which was supported by a powerful, resilient love. It was this love that communicated itself to us with such force that it almost appeared to exist in a tangible form. Within this context, the assertion that 'God is Love' began to have real meaning.

Since childhood, my own internal image of God had been a hazy amalgamation of a benevolent old gentleman and a gigantic genie of the lamp. But now, I could discern within this body of people at West Street a unity based on belief and a deep love for one another which was recognisable as the Spirit of God. Our acceptance and welcome as fellow Christians by the other church members inspired us and we were warmed by a powerful current of love. The excitement of this new life illuminated our lives.

* * *

However, I soon discovered that the same power which activated loving relationships and gave unity to a group of dissimilar people, was also able to reveal personal defects and weaknesses. I began to recognise that my behaviour was often dominated by self-interest. And there was a superficiality in my relationships with others that prevented me from being truly caring towards them.

A vague awareness of this condition was brought into focus by a series of incidents that happened over a period of weeks. During one conversation with Mike Wood, I was being very critical of other local churches and comparing them unfavourably with West Street. At the end of my lengthy condemnation, Mike's gentle reply felt like a rapier thrust into my heart.

"We are all trying to serve the same God," he said quietly. "We have to learn to help and co-operate with others."

As Mike spoke, I suddenly became aware of the critical attitude deep within me. For years, it had enjoyed complete freedom, quietly doing its destructive work – identifying and observing the bad in others, drawing attention to other people's weaknesses and inabilities. In that instant, I realised that it was a part of my personality that was incompatible with God's Spirit. This unexpected revelation caused me heartache for days, and for weeks afterwards every critical word I uttered rang out like an alarm bell.

Another valuable lesson was learned from an elderly lady, a regular member of the congregation. In conversation one Sunday morning, I mentioned a Summer Fair which was to be held on the following Saturday at the school where I was head teacher. I flippantly suggested that any help she was able to give would be very welcome as we were short of stall-holders. I did not take the lady's offer to 'see if she could make it' seriously and the whole episode had slipped from my mind before I left the church.

Imagine my surprise on the following Sunday morning to find myself accepting an apology from the dear old soul. She told me that she had not been well and had not been able to help at the fair. I mumbled some suitable words to cover my embarrassment, but later I thought about what had happened.

The point that struck home was that the old lady had meant what she said. I had not. My request for help had been flippant. Not for one moment had I expected her to make the difficult journey to my school and help with the fair. But I had asked – and she had intended to respond. The lesson was clear. In relationships which exist under God, there is no place for half-truths or insincerity.

Through incidents such as these, Anita and I found that our lives were gradually being changed. We began to see everyday events through new eyes; we were drawn into more loving relationships; we developed openness with other people. Our everyday world was perceived through an altered consciousness – and we were happier than ever before.

* * *

Anita decided to be baptised soon after we joined 'West Street'. A baptismal service had been arranged for 29th May 1977, and she asked Mike if she could be baptised with the two other candidates on that day.

I held back. Although I felt sure that this should be my next step too, I could not summon up enough courage to make the firm decision.

"Plenty of time," I reasoned. "No point in jumping in with both feet!"

The phrase encapsulated my apprehension. Baptism by total immersion is a physical as well as a spiritual experience, and I found the prospect of submitting to a ducking before a hundred or so people overwhelming.

When the day of the baptismal service arrived Anita was calm and composed. Even when Mike invited her to join him at the front of the church she showed few signs of nervousness. Mike led her gently through her testimony and the baptism took place. After the service the congregation gathered in the church lounge for coffee. There was a buzz of excitement as members came to hug and congratulate Anita, and she was filled by a sense of well-being.

I felt disappointed that I had missed an opportunity. I decided to be baptised on the next appropriate occasion and, during the days that followed, my confidence and enthusiasm grew. Within a week I had bought a small lapel badge – a cross – and had begun to wear it in my jacket. It was a simple act of witness that seemed to demand from me an enormous amount of courage.

By the time Sunday 17th July dawned – the day of *my* baptism – I had been through a testing time. During the past two or three weeks, deep waves of doubt had swept over me, and I had been aware of a continuous battle going on within. When I weighed the evidence *intellectually,* I began to wonder if I was involved in some sort of self-delusion, but there were other times when the joy of my new life welled up inside me, causing my spirit to soar with happiness and gratitude.

However, when the time came for me to join Mike in the baptistry, I knew I was doing the right thing. I had to go forward in faith – there could be no turning back. We stood almost waist deep in the water as Mike asked me his final question:

"Rod, do you confess that Jesus Christ is your Saviour and Lord, and do you promise to serve him and follow him and love him always?"

"I do."

There was a pause for prayer, and several members of the congregation read out appropriate verses of scripture. Then I felt Mike's grip on the front of my shirt tighten, and became aware of his other arm supporting my back. The moment of baptism had arrived. Mike's voice was firm and clear.

"On your confession that Jesus Christ is your Saviour and Lord and on your promise to serve him and follow him and love him always, I baptise you, with joy, in the name of the Father, and of the Son, and of the Holy Spirit. Amen."

PART THREE

Unexpected Journeys

Chapter Twenty-six

New Christians

Following my baptism at West Street Baptist Church in July 1977, I didn't sit around waiting for God to give me something to do. I had a school to run! The end of the Summer Term in primary schools is always busy and this was no exception. There were pre-admission visits by new pupils to be organized, teachers' reports to be read and signed, parents' evenings to be arranged, a sports day to plan and a thousand other tasks to be performed to bring the school year to a satisfactory conclusion. On some days my feet hardly touched the ground!

At West Street, Anita and I gradually became more involved in the life of the Church. Within months we had been accepted into Church membership, and began to take an active part in the activities that went on there.

Beneath the worship centre was a large rambling cellar which had been cleared out and transformed into a Christian Coffee Cellar by a group of young people from the church. It opened every Saturday evening and welcomed everybody, including many young people who would not have been seen dead in a church service! A series of concerts and events was arranged and often there was standing room only as a popular Christian singer performed, or a young evangelist gave his message.

Anita offered to help with serving refreshments – mainly coffee, biscuits and chocolate bars – and was soon co-opted on to the Church Catering Team. She had always had an interest in drama, and was thrilled to join the Christian Drama Group which performed sketches during services, or gave performances at other churches or special events.

After a few months, Mike Wood asked me if I would be willing to join the diaconate, the group of church members who supervise the running of the church. I agreed to stand for the office, was elected, and not long after took on the post of Church Secretary, writing minutes of the monthly meetings and dealing with all the correspondence.

Our children enjoyed being part of the West Street family as much as we did. Lisa persuaded her friend Justine – who lived close by – to come with us on Sunday mornings and they took part in all the activities that were arranged for their age group. Lisa was twice chosen to be a bridesmaid by young women of the church, and enjoyed being part of their special day. So life was quite exciting for her.

David became firm friends with Mark and Ian, Mike Wood's boys, and the three of them spent hours practising on their guitars and working out programmes for their Christian rock group "Open Door" to perform at church events. Once they were even asked to play at an old folks' Christmas party!

As a family, we supported Traidcraft events, and helped to run Church barbecues and weekends away. Sometimes, too, we gave hospitality to missionaries, singers or speakers who were visiting the church.

As Mike often said, "Living a Christian life may be tiring, even exhausting, but it's never boring!"

* * *

1978 was Mike Wood's sabbatical year, when he was due a period of study leave. The church members surprised him with the gift of a holiday – a visit to the Holy Land, fulfilling a long held wish. When at the end of a social evening, arranged to celebrate Mike's years of service, he was let into the secret, he was not only deeply touched but over the moon with joy.

Over the next few weeks Mike shared with everyone his excitement at the prospect of the visit and wondered how he was going to fit everything he needed to take in his suitcase! He knew he was to travel with a group of Christians from all denominations who were making a pilgrimage to Israel and he intended to see, learn and record everything he could. After what was a marvellous week for him, Mike returned to Rochdale loaded down with photographic slides, artefacts and anecdotes. The visit had had a profound effect on him and he wanted to share his experiences with the church that had so lovingly sent him.

A week or so later an 'Israel Evening' was arranged. There Mike explained the locations and described the various sites as his photo slides were flashed up on the screen. At the end of the evening he made an announcement.

"This has been such a wonderful experience for me that I would like all of you to share it," he said. "I have sat on the hillside where Jesus delivered his sermon on the mount; I have seen the beggars at the Damascus Gate in Jerusalem; I have strolled through the busy market place, and I have watched the fishermen, like St. Peter, fishing in the Sea of Galilee. Next year, I would like to take a group from West Street to see all these sights for themselves."

Mike went on to explain that if more than twenty people booked on the trip, he would be entitled to a free place and would come as our spiritual guide to lead us around Jerusalem and take us to the sites described in the bible. Everyone was thrilled by the idea and many people, especially the younger folk, made plans to put aside a little money each week to pay for the trip.

Anita and I decided that we couldn't possibly go to Israel. As I've said before, we were a naturally cautious couple. And what is more we had a mortgage to pay and a growing family to rear! We had managed to save almost £1,000 over the years but it would take all of that to pay for the trip. We would have nothing to fall back on in case of emergency. We talked it over and much to David and Lisa's disappointment, decided that it would not be sensible.

However, there was an even stronger reason for staying at home – Anita was terrified of flying. Although she had never flown, for years she had had a recurrent nightmare of being in an aeroplane that was about to crash. She would wake up in sheer terror as the vivid dream jerked her into consciousness. Realistically speaking there was no way she would even consider going in an aeroplane – the very thought of it brought her out in a cold sweat! Ages ago we had reached the conclusion that we would never be able to fly abroad – it was too much to ask of Anita. We asserted that there were lots of beautiful places in the United Kingdom we had not visited!

Several months passed, and there was mounting excitement in the Church as the date of the pilgrimage drew closer. The time came for final payments to be made and bookings to be finalized.

Within days of the deadline, I woke up one morning convinced we were doing the wrong thing. We were making a mistake. We should go. I felt wary of sharing these thoughts with Anita, but she did not react in the way I had expected. Instead of protesting that I was going back on our agreement, she supported my idea. She argued that we had always planned carefully, risked nothing and been self-reliant, so perhaps now was the time to follow our hearts rather than our heads and join the pilgrimage. When I asked how she would cope with the flight, she said that with the support of our West Street family she was sure everything would be alright!

Our children were delighted that we had changed our minds and David couldn't wait to pick up the telephone and tell Mark and Ian Wood the good news. Since forming their Christian Rock Group they had become inseparable.

At 6 a.m. on Saturday 17th February 1979, we joined the party of twenty-five people – married couples, children and single adults – which left a snow-covered Rochdale by coach to head southwards on the M6 motorway. Despite the wintry conditions, we arrived safely at Heathrow at 11 a.m., unloaded our baggage and went through into the departure lounge. It was all very strange to us as we had never before spent time in an airport, so we found plenty to do and see to keep us occupied until it was time for our plane to leave.

When our flight was eventually called, we all made our way down the covered gangway into the plane. Anita was feeling pretty wobbly by this time but she was on the plane itself before she knew it. The plane was a jumbo jet and our seats were in the middle section – thankfully away from any windows! We seemed to sit for ages before being given permission to take off but finally the engines roared into life. Anita was terrified by the loud noise but Lisa and I, sitting on either side of her, took hold of her hands and Mike Wood, on the row behind, reached forward and placed his hand on her shoulder. I could hear him praying quietly.

As the plane raced down the runway, Anita sat rigid with fear, tears running silently down her cheeks, but as we soared into the sky she began to relax and after fifteen minutes or so, felt more at ease. Because it was a four hour flight the company, El Al, served two full meals as well as orange juice and duty-free sales so Anita was kept far too occupied to worry much about being 50,000 feet in the air!

Three and half hours later as we began the descent into Tel Aviv airport, Anita's anxiety returned, but thankfully we had a soft landing and soon we were walking down the steps of the aircraft into the warm balmy air of an Israeli evening.

Our week in Israel was both eventful and memorable. The first four days were spent in the Strand Hotel in Jerusalem. From there we moved on to Nazareth, to stay in the Beit Sprinzak, a far smarter modern hotel which boasted every facility but was lacking in personal warmth, care and humanity.

Every day of our visit was packed with activity. We explored religious sites – the Mount of Olives, the Pool of Bethsaida and the Garden of Gethsemene – and we walked along the Via Dolorosa, the Way of the Cross. We bought fruit in the bustling bazaar, had a meal at a Kibbutz, and visited the Shepherd's fields and the Church of the Nativity in Bethlehem. Our guide explained that many of the sites were 'traditional,' and that there was no way of proving they were the places where the events had actually happened. In fact, in some cases there were two sites dedicated to the same episode, and we all agreed that not even Jesus could have ascended into heaven from two places simultaneously!

Throughout the week our group was just like one large extended family. We talked together, ate together, walked together, shared jokes together and prayed together. Perhaps the most important thing we learned was that the Israeli culture was very different from our own and this knowledge enabled us to gain new insights into passages from the bible. It was now much easier to imagine the scene as Jesus healed the blind beggar at the roadside – for we saw several of them on our trip. We now knew what sort of men the disciples were, for we watched fishermen on Lake Galilee using the same methods they had used for centuries.

We found it disappointing that many of the Christian sites were covered by huge, ornate basilicas which seemed to contrast sharply with the humility and simplicity of Christ's lifestyle and message. It felt wrong to be walking across mosaic pavements and through gold-lined, bejewelled passageways to see the supposed site of a simple manger. It was confusing to find Jesus' empty tomb in the undercroft of a vast, highly decorated church guarded by a sombre black-robed priest.

By contrast we found another site, the Garden Tomb – an ancient burial place carved in a rock face within a garden – to be more authentic, and to convey more of the crucifixion story to us than the riches of the Church of the Holy Sepulchre.

The week passed all too quickly, and everyone was sad as the end of the holiday drew near. The visit had given us the opportunity to draw even closer as a church family, and we knew we would have many happy memories to treasure.

As the pilgrimage came to an end, Anita had to face the worrying prospect of the return flight. However, encouraged by the group, her anxiety was far less than on the outward journey, and she arrived back at Heathrow with a great sense of achievement. Her phobia would no longer govern our travel plans.

Once back home, we were eager to tell our friends, family, and colleagues all about our pilgrimage to Israel. We were full of the excitement of it all!

We recognized too that Anita's phobia could well have kept us at home, denying us the experience of a lifetime. We knew that it had been the loving support and acceptance of our West Street family that had enabled her to face up to her fear and overcome it. For us, this was yet another miracle.

Chapter Twenty-seven

The Whole Story

In 1980, a Borough-wide Christian festival was to be held in Rochdale. After a period of prayer and discussion, a team of local ministers headed by Mike Wood had decided to ask Canon David Watson, of St. Michael-le-Belfry Church in York to lead a Celebration and Mission in the town. This was to take place in early spring and had the support of fifty-two local churches of all denominations.

Of course, West Street was involved in all the preparations and arrangements and Anita and I were particularly excited to hear that St. Michael's, which had played such an important part in our conversion to Christianity, was to lead the celebration.

The mission was to be called:

THE WHOLE STORY – FESTIVAL 80 – FOR THE WHOLE OF ROCHDALE.

It was planned that groups and committees should be set up to oversee different aspects of the festival. There was to be:

- A Festival of Praise – comprising a series of evening celebrations led by Reverend David Watson and his team from York.
- Young People's Days – events and activities aimed at young Christians, youth groups, etc.
- Performances by 'Riding Lights', the professional theatre company made up of Christians that had recently won a 'first' at the Edinburgh Festival Fringe – the same group that Anita and I had seen in the courtyard off Stonegate in 1976.

- An Oratorio Choir, comprising local Christians from every denomination.
- A modern Christian musical: 'Come Together', to be sung by a choir of around seventy Christians which would tour churches of all denominations across the Borough.

Anita and I were looking forward to the event and became part of the General Committee responsible for preparation, planning and organization. In addition, Anita joined the Drama Group and the 'Come Together' choir.

Everyone at West Street was buzzing with excitement as the Festival drew near – there were rehearsals to attend, hospitality to be provided, printed material to be sent out to churches and schools, and many practical issues to resolve. When the Festival began eighty churches were involved.

The main events of 'The Whole Story' took place during the week 18th to 23rd March and everyone agreed that it was a resounding success. The Central Methodist Hall in Rochdale (Champness Hall) was filled to capacity and closed-circuit television was used to relay events to people who could not get into the main auditorium. During the Festival, and for many months afterwards, several churches in the area sprang to life with creativity and became willing to try out new things in their services.

* * *

At around this time, I noticed that Anita was occasionally holding her wrist or rubbing her shoulder. When I asked her about it she replied rather hesitantly that they were 'a bit stiff'. My anxiety aroused, I watched her carefully over the next few days and began to fear the worst – that after almost two pain-free years, her arthritis was returning!

My spirits sank. Over the next few weeks I became at first depressed and then angry. I was like a bear with a sore head! Whenever I spoke to Anita about it, she seemed to prevaricate, never giving a straight answer to a straight question.

"I don't know if it is arthritis," she would say impatiently in response to my continual questioning, "I just feel an ache in my joints sometimes."

It was as though she was trying to protect me from despair by denying that the illness had returned.

When finally Anita visited our G.P. he referred her once again to the Rheumatism Clinic at Manchester Royal Infirmary. After tests, they confirmed that there were some signs of active arthritis, but they were not sure if it was the same form of arthritis that she had had before.

Instead of being encouraging and supportive I became despondent. I didn't feel able to cope with the idea that Anita's arthritis had recurred. It seemed to throw into doubt everything that had happened over the past two years. I felt like the victim of a gigantic confidence trick – one played on me by none other than God!

Anita's approach was much more rational. She had had a long period of remission for which she was very grateful. She had promised God that if he took away the illness, she would never doubt him again and she did not intend to do so. And anyway, there was no such thing as permanent healing. Even those people whom Jesus healed had died eventually because that is the nature of life on earth.

Despite her arguments, I felt cheated. I shared my feelings of disappointment, anger and despair with Mike Wood, who admitted that he had no answer for me. This was one occasion when we had to trust God and believe that everything would turn out for good in the end.

* * *

As the weeks passed by, although Anita was not in as much pain as she had been a few years before, I could see a change in her as she moved around the house. She had little strength in her joints and had become less free in her movements.

I had become less free in my movements too! Becoming a Christian had brought a greater sense of freedom into my life. Having grown up in a family where there was not much physical contact, I had always felt awkward if I had to greet anyone with a kiss, or give them a hug on their birthday. At West Street, these inhibitions had disappeared, and I had found freedom to express myself physically as well as verbally.

With the return of Anita's arthritis, I switched off from everyone and drew back into my shell. My open, accepting attitude changed to cynicism and I began to look upon any piece of good news with suspicion.

Whether or not my scepticism was justified I do not know, but my cynical attitude was not helpful to me or to anyone else. Instead of being filled with love, I began to develop a judgemental attitude, belittling other's experiences. And as I did so, I gradually cut myself off from the love and joy which surrounded me and became withdrawn and melancholy.

I drifted along like this for some time until I realised there was an important question I had to answer: 'Would you rather be right, or happy?' Part of me asserted that I would prefer to be right, but I began to realise that I didn't know that I was right! For if a stranger were to meet Anita at this point in our lives and hear her tell of how she had been miraculously healed, he would not believe it. And yet she and I knew that it was true – it had happened – and had been a very real event in our lives.

After weeks of heart-searching, I came to recognise that there were many things beyond my understanding. How was it, for instance, that some people, given six months to live, were still enjoying life six years later, whilst others, who had never had a day's illness in their lives, suddenly passed away in their sleep? And what about other aspects of life which could never be proved scientifically? How could one 'prove', for example, that one was loved, trusted, valued, forgiven – yet these were some of the most valuable gifts one could ever receive in life.

I sat down and reflected on everything that had happened to us over the last few years: Anita's years of remission from pain; our coming to faith by such different routes; the loving supportive fellowship that our family were now so much a part of; our inspiring holiday in Israel; the joy of being part of the Rochdale Festival and the fact that I had felt happier and more fulfilled than at any other time in my life.

I knew that I had to follow Mike Wood's advice. I had to trust God and believe that He would make sure that everything turned out for good in the end.

Chapter Twenty-eight

Passion Play

Whilst I was absorbed in my crisis of faith, Anita was getting on with life. The Passion Play in Oberammergau in Germany, performed every ten years, was due to take place during the Summer of 1980 and, freed from her flying phobia, Anita decided she would like to go!

She mentioned this to one or two people at West Street and several expressed an interest. We made enquiries with a travel agent and armed with brochures and application forms, we announced to the church that we would organize the visit. Imagine our disappointment when only five people actually signed up to go with us – all of them elderly! How would David and Lisa, now aged 15 and 13, enjoy such an experience, we wondered?

The travel agent explained that visits to the Passion Play were included within a week's holiday at another centre. We would have an overnight stay as house-guests in the home of a local family before the performance, and for the rest of the week we would be booked into a hotel in another resort – in our case, Kitzbuhel in Austria.

At 5.50 a.m. on Saturday 2nd August we climbed aboard the minibus which was to take us to Manchester Airport. The party consisted of Arthur and Alice, a married couple in their seventies; Phyllis, a widow of a similar age; Lily, the elderly church caretaker and her sister, Violet. Although I tried to look on the bright side, a fun-packed holiday did not seem to be on the cards!

I could not have been more wrong! From the moment we arrived at Munich Airport, we had adventure after adventure. As we left the airport we discovered that a stranger had picked up Arthur's suitcase from the carousel by mistake and was disappearing with it through the exit. We raced through a crowded concourse to recover it from the very apologetic traveller, before shepherding our inexperienced group onto the coach that was to take us to Ettal, where our overnight hosts lived – only to find ourselves on a circular tour as the driver didn't seem to know where he was going!

When we eventually arrived at our destination, Anita and I had to find the houses of our various hosts and introduce their 'guests' to them. As none of us could speak a word of German and our hosts spoke very little English this was not an easy matter, but we managed with the help of lots of smiles and gestures.

The lady of the house where our family was staying, Frau Steffl, showed us to a pair of beautifully appointed rooms with balconies overlooking breathtaking views of the surrounding countryside.

Later, when we all met in the centre of Ettal, we learned that everyone was delighted with their accommodation. We wandered through sunlit streets and came upon a café bar which sold delicious gateaux and ice cream, so we decided to give ourselves a treat. It was only when we worked out the exchange rate that we realised it had cost as much as a three course meal in England!

The following day a coach took us to the picturesque village of Oberammergau and we saw the immense theatre where the performance was to take place. Originally, the play had been performed in the streets of the village, but in recent years a large auditorium had been built to protect the audience from bad weather. However, the enormous stage was in the open air and the actors were still exposed to the elements.

The presentation of the Passion Play was superb. It began early in the morning and there was a three hour interval at midday during which everyone went into the village to an allotted restaurant to eat lunch – vouchers had been included with the holiday tickets. As the play was in German, we had each bought an English translation, but this was not really necessary as we were all very familiar with the story.

Some of the scenes were truly spectacular! On Palm Sunday, vast numbers of people, including children and babes in arms, thronged on to the stage with palm branches and cried out to Jesus as he rode to Jerusalem on the back of a donkey. When Jesus cleansed the Temple, flocks of pigeons were released, lambs raced across the stage, pots were shattered and coins rolled across the floor as tables were overturned. In other scenes, Roman soldiers on horseback galloped back and forth, their hooves pounding the stage beneath them. The trial of Jesus and the crucifixion were very realistic and emotional, and we all emerged during the late afternoon moved and impressed by all we had seen.

The day ended with a long coach journey to the Hotel Tyrol in Kitzbuhel, a 'chocolate-box' chalet with balconies and geranium-filled window boxes. Our bedroom was on the third floor – and there was no lift. But the panoramic view of the town and the mountain peaks beyond more than made up for the climb!

* * *

Our party of nine got on remarkably well together. The older folk felt secure because they knew we would help to sort out any minor problems they had; David and Lisa had five 'adopted' grandparents who enjoyed their chatter and spoilt them with ice creams and other treats; Anita and I had far more freedom than usual as our children were not always with us.

During the week, we shared in some activities and did others separately. Lisa discovered the 'Aquarena' Adventure Pool complex, complete with wave and bubble machine – something unknown in Britain at the time – and she and David spent many happy hours there. We sat enjoying the sunshine in the gardens nearby, occasionally walking over to wave to them both through the observation window.

One afternoon the whole party set off to ride on the cable car. As we approached the embarkation platform and saw the cables soaring high towards the mountain top, Lily and Violet – who weren't keen on heights – took fright. They decided to stay in the valley but the rest of us bravely stepped aboard and made the smooth ascent to the summit. There we sat on the observation terrace viewing the valley far below and gasping in amazement as a team of hang gliders launched themselves out over the tree tops and wheeled and glided on the rising currents of air.

On another day we went on an excursion to Saltsburg. Our coach picked us up at 8.00 a.m. and we set out along a road that wound through spectacular scenery. We stopped at Berchtesgaden, Hitler's 'Eagle's Nest' where he had his infamous conference with Chamberlain, and paused by a lake to take photographs of the large country house beyond, in which 'The Sound of Music' had been filmed.

When we returned to Kitzbuhel we all felt rather tired, but as we had booked seats for a Tyrolean concert at the Praxmair Café Bar that evening, there was little time to recover. At the Praxmair we crowded together around a vacant table in an alcove and settled down to enjoy the entertainment. A group of sixteen men and women in national costume appeared on stage with a small Tyrolean band and began to perform traditional dances. Although they moved skilfully, their dancing lacked joy and spontaneity. They performed automatically without a hint of pleasure on their faces. We all decided, on reflection, that we might have been better off resting in our hotel!

And so the week went by. Our West Street party had lots of conversations, shared jokes together and spent a good deal of time laughing. It was my birthday whilst we were away and I was surprised and pleased to come down to breakfast one morning to be greeted by the strains of 'Happy Birthday to You'. Phyllis stood up and gave a speech of congratulation and thanked Anita and me for organising the trip, which she followed by presenting me with a birthday gift of a Tyrolean hat, complete with feather!

Long after we had all returned to Rochdale, our group of five elderly companions spoke in glowing terms of their visit to Oberammergau and the holiday in Kitzbuhel that followed. Anita and I began making regular visits to see Arthur and Alice in their home and they were always glad to see us. They had no children or close relatives, so as long as they were able to do so, we invited them to join our family parties during the Christmas season.

Even many years later, when they had both become very old and frail, they spent hours reminiscing with us about their Austrian holiday, saying that it was the most exciting and memorable adventure they had ever undertaken in their entire lives.

Chapter Twenty-nine

Marriage Encounter

At the end of the summer term in 1981, I found myself – as usual at this time of the school year – running to keep up with myself! One morning, in the midst of the hectic end-of-term programme, there was a tap on my office door and a familiar face peeped round the edge of it.

"Could I have a word?" asked my visitor.

My caller was Wray Buckley, a Health Visitor with whom I had regular contact. She often came into school to report on children's health matters, or to give me information about a family who were going through a difficult time.

I invited her to take a seat.

Wray wanted to have a conversation with me about the eleven-year-old girls in our top class who were due to leave the school.

"Children are maturing much earlier these days," she said, "and some of the girls are already growing into young women. I would like them to see a film explaining what is happening to their bodies before they move on to secondary school."

I looked at her in amazement.

"Wray, there is only *one week* to go before we close for the holiday, and you know I couldn't allow pupils to see a film like that without my seeing it first. Some parents are very sensitive and might object..."

"I've thought of that," she interrupted. "It only lasts for about fifteen minutes, and I would set it up on the projector at the Health Centre. When everything is ready, I could come and collect you in my car and bring you back straight afterwards...."

"Alright," I sighed reluctantly, "How about tomorrow morning? We could show it to the girls later in the week."

Wray smiled. "I thought you'd agree," she said, as she left my office.

At ten o'clock next morning, a car pulled up on the school car park and Wray stepped out of it. I had been keeping an eye out for her through my office window, so I set off and met her at the front door. As we got into her car and drove off, she pointed to a transparent car sticker affixed to her windscreen.

"Do you know what that is?" she asked.

I glanced at it, noting a red heart with circles beneath. As Wray was a nurse I assumed it was connected with giving blood, but she soon corrected me.

"It's the Marriage Encounter symbol," she said. "It's a Christian movement designed to strengthen marriages. Its motto is 'Make your Good Marriage Great'. Couples go away together to a conference centre for a weekend to work on their marriages. My husband and I are part of the Anglican Marriage Encounter team."

I wasn't sure why she was telling me this.

"My wife and I already have a good marriage," I replied, "and in any case, I wouldn't want to discuss our relationship in front of others."

"It *is* for good marriages," emphasised Wray, "and the weekend is entirely private. The Team Couples – who lead the weekend – talk about various aspects of their own relationship and then the couples on the weekend leave to discuss the same area – in complete privacy."

"And it's an Anglican course?"

"Well, it began within the Catholic Church, but a few years ago the Anglicans took it up. It's actually for all Christians..."

By this time, we had arrived at the Health Centre, so our conversation came to an end. I was shown the film and agreed that it was suitable for our girl leavers to watch, but on the way back Wray resumed our conversation.

"Marriage Encounter weekends are usually held in hotels, and if you'd like a list of dates, I could let you have one..."

"We actually go to a Baptist Church," I interrupted, hoping to stem her flow. But she persisted.

"Well, that's great! The Baptists are planning to hold their very first weekend any time now. I'll get you the telephone number of the couple who are organising it; then if you are interested you can give them a ring."

We arrived back at school, and thanking Wray for the lift, I returned to the many tasks still awaiting me. However throughout the day the conversation about Marriage Encounter kept running through my mind, and when I got home I decided to share it with Anita. I explained that the weekends were intended for good marriages, were completely private, and were usually held in hotels.

"So I was wondering if we should book on a weekend," I concluded. "How do you fancy the idea?"

Anita was surprised by my suggestion, but soon agreed that after twenty years of marriage and raising our children, perhaps we deserved a couple of days' relaxation in a comfortable hotel together.

The following evening, I rang the telephone number which Wray had dropped into school that day, and found myself speaking to Brenda Reynolds who lived with her husband Bill over 200 miles away in Chesham, Buckinghamshire. There was a slight hesitation in her voice when I asked if I could make a booking, but she said she would put an information pack and an application form in the post on the following day.

What Anita and I didn't know then was that our telephone call was the catalyst that prompted Bill and Brenda to spring into action. A weekend had been provisionally arranged but the details had not yet been finalised.

The Reynolds had been introduced to Marriage Encounter during the previous year by one of Brenda's colleagues at work, and they had booked on an Anglican weekend which had been held in Lowestoft. They had found the two-day experience so helpful that they were keen to introduce the movement into the Baptist Church. But as they didn't know how to move forward, they contacted the Baptist Marriage Encounter leadership in America to get advice.

Then, another of those strange 'coincidences' occurred. At precisely the same time, Reverend Norman Barr, pastor of Leighton Buzzard Baptist Church, was on sabbatical leave in America. During his final two weeks he had been joined by his wife, Eirlys. Within those two weeks, at Eirlys' instigation, the couple had attended an American Marriage Encounter weekend and thought it so valuable that they too wanted to introduce it into their own denomination in England.

So the Barrs and the Reynolds were introduced to each other by the American leadership – and discovered they lived only ten miles apart in England! Soon after Norman and Eirlys returned home, the two couples met and discussed their shared vision. After further training, they set about preparing the necessary material and arranging the venue for the first ever British Baptist Marriage Encounter weekend.

They had invited four couples from their own churches in Leighton Buzzard and Chesham to attend, and two American couples had agreed to fly in to help when all the arrangements had been finalised. It was thought that a suitable venue might be the Watermill Moat House Hotel in Berkhamsted.

It was at this point, out of the blue, that an unknown couple from 'up north' rang to book a place on the weekend and Baptist Marriage Encounter became a reality!

* * *

On Friday 16th October 1981, I left school promptly at 4.00 p.m. and an hour later Anita and I were driving down the M1 motorway on our way south. We were embarking on a three-and-a-half hour journey to an unfamiliar destination for an unknown experience!

We drove into the hotel car park and were greeted by willing helpers who took our cases and carried them into the hotel and up to our comfortable en-suite bedroom. They led us into the lounge where we were given a warm welcome and offered coffee and refreshments. However, a little later, when the programme for the weekend was explained to us we were in for a shock. We soon realised it was to be a highly disciplined, hard-working time devoted to exploring and sharing every aspect of our relationship. Afterwards, Anita jokingly referred to our time there as being a cross between a monastery and a boot camp!

Nevertheless, during the next forty-four hours Anita and I shared thoughts and feelings which we had kept hidden for years – sometimes even from ourselves. Prompted by the example of the team couples, and in the safe environment they had created, we learned new ways of communicating with each other and expressing our fears, uncertainties, hopes and dreams. By the end of the weekend it seemed as if we had a renewed marriage.

Then came a final shock. As we were about to leave on the long journey home on Sunday evening, the team members asked to speak with us. They said that they had been watching us over the weekend, and the strength of our relationship had shone through. They believed that God was calling us to be part of the Baptist Marriage Encounter Team. It would involve us in preparing talks and helping to lead weekends all over the United Kingdom. Would we think and pray about this over the next twenty-four hours, and they would ring us on Monday evening to ask for our decision.

There was not a moment of silence on our journey home – we had so much to think about and discuss. Although we arrived home exhausted, we didn't get much sleep that night. But by the following evening, both Anita and I had come to the same conclusion. We had the necessary experience. We had faced and come through some difficult early years in our marriage; we had successfully raised two children – now in their teens; we had both come to faith independently and were supported within a warm, loving church. Although we had not sought this Christian work, we knew we were well equipped to do it. So when we received the expected phone call on the Monday evening, there was only one answer we could give. We agreed to join the team.

Chapter Thirty

Preparing for the Work

E arly in 1982, the Baptist Marriage Encounter Team consisted of just three couples: Reverend Norman and Eirlys Barr, Bill and Brenda Reynolds, and ourselves – the most recent recruits. A complete Marriage Encounter team should have four couples – one of which has to be a Pastoral couple – to spread the workload, but we all decided to prepare the necessary material between us, so that our Baptist Team could operate for a while with one couple short. However, before we could begin writing, Anita and I had to attend a further Anglican weekend, which took us deeper into the dynamics of the marriage relationship. This behind us, we started writing in earnest.

We soon realised that it was going to be a very demanding task. The talks covered a variety of topics pertaining to marriage, and had to contain true and relevant examples from the Couple's own relationship. The theory was that because the Team Couples were open and honest in talking about their difficulties and uncertainties, the couples on the weekend would feel able to be open and honest with each other in the privacy of their rooms.

Our talks not only had to follow an 'outline' in order to dovetail with those of other Team Couples, they also had to be open and frank, revealing intimate and personal details about our relationship. Whilst we did not find talking about our family finances too threatening, revealing our attitudes and expectations in love-making or child-rearing made us feel very vulnerable. Yet, we both knew from our own weekend experience that it was this public openness and vulnerability in the Team Couples that had encouraged us to share deeply together in private.

As each talk was completed we had to send it away to an experienced Anglican Marriage Encounter couple for checking and editing. More often than not it was returned covered in pencil marks and accompanied by a number of suggestions, comments and amendments. Sometimes we had wandered away from the topic and included sections that were irrelevant, at other times we had made the material interesting but managed to avoid mentioning a key aspect because it was difficult to share!

At the time of our writing, computers were not in general use, so any material returned had to be re-typed – or in our case re-written – and then submitted afresh to the editing couple. Sometimes the material went back and forth three times before it was passed as 'satisfactory'.

Throughout this time, which covered many weeks, Anita and I did not doubt for a moment that we were doing the right thing. We worked hard on our talks every Saturday morning, rising early and often continuing into the early afternoon.

Gradually as the weeks and months passed by, we assembled a portfolio of 'approved' material, until we had enough talks for us to be able to take part in a weekend.

During the whole time we were writing, we had kept in touch with Bill and Brenda Reynolds – indeed they had travelled north on one occasion and stayed with us for a couple of days. We found we got on very well together and shared many hilarious 'northerners' versus 'southerners' jokes. We knew that we were engaged in an important Christian work together and over the next few years became close friends.

It was decided that our reduced team of three Team Couples could probably manage to run three weekends during the first year and leaflets and application forms were produced accordingly. However, as the Anglicans had been running their weekends primarily in the south of England, the initial demand for Baptist Weekends was in the south too, so naturally venues were chosen which were convenient for most of the applicants. A favourite hotel was the Watermill Moat House Hotel in

Berkhamsted, which had comfortable accommodation, a good conference room and friendly, helpful staff.

Of course this meant that Anita and I had to drive 230 miles on busy Friday evenings in order to get to the venue by 7.30 p.m., when the weekend presentations were due to begin. I would leave school at the earliest possible moment – five minutes after the end of school – and drive home to find Anita waiting in the hallway with a flask of coffee, sandwiches and a suitcase containing our clothes.

She would hurry into the car, we would ask a blessing on our journey, and then set off for the motorway, heading south. It may be another 'coincidence', but although we often saw three lanes of traffic tailing back for several miles on the opposite carriageway, never once were we delayed on our way to a Marriage Encounter Weekend. During those early years we were scheduled to give the very first talk: "Introduction to the Weekend" and never once were we late.

Whichever Faith Group runs a Marriage Encounter weekend – Catholics, Anglicans or Baptists – the outline of the talks is similar. But of course every weekend is also truly unique in that it is the personal sharings of each team couple that illustrate the points being made. There may well be differences in style which reflect the ethos of each denomination, but essentially all Weekends are aimed at strengthening marriages which are already sound.

The most important element of the weekend is the introduction of a method of communication in which couples learn to be empathic and understanding even if a partner's views or feelings do not coincide with their own. They are given some tips on how to have arguments – even full-blown rows – without breaking the relationship or causing deep hurts.

By the end of the first year, with three or four weekends under our belt, our Baptist Team of three couples began to feel more confident. We had seen some amazing transformations in the lives of couples who had booked on weekends, and even though there was no obligation to share anything with the Team, several of them had told us that for the first time in their lives they had begun to understand how their partners 'ticked'. Some even said they had fallen in love with their spouse all over again!

The weekends were by no means filled with young or newly married couples – indeed it was recommended that couples did not attend a weekend until they had been married for at least two years. Often there were middle-aged couples, who seemed to benefit greatly, and on more than one occasion we were privileged to share the weekend with couples celebrating their silver, ruby, or even golden wedding anniversaries.

After a year or so, our Team of Three felt drawn to one of the couples who had attended a weekend – their relationship seemed to overflow with all the qualities of love and care that are essential in a marriage. So we approached Harford and Jenny Smith from Oxfordshire and asked them to consider joining us in the work – and they readily agreed to do so. On a later weekend, another couple, with similar qualities, were invited to become team members and we were delighted that Howard and Kathy Ward from Hertfordshire decided to join us.

Both couples went on to further training and began writing their talks, just as we had done a couple of years before. This time, instead of relying on an Anglican couple to check and edit them, Norman and Eirlys, and Bill and Brenda asked us to take on the task.

Thus a new area of work came our way. Although by now we had written all our own presentations, our Saturday mornings were once again fully occupied as we checked – or "workshopped" – talks written by other couples.

Gradually, the Baptist Marriage Encounter Team began to grow and applications for weekend places came from more northerly locations. We found suitable venues in Wales, the Midlands and even in Lancashire and Yorkshire!

Because we now had more Team Couples, it was not always necessary for us to make the dash to Berkhamsted on Friday afternoons. We were able to have the occasional southern weekend off and put our efforts into workshopping and organising the northern weekends. However, in order to be able to form two separate teams, which we would have liked to do, we needed to recruit another Pastoral couple. Although several ministers and their wives had attended our weekends, and found them personally beneficial, none had felt specifically 'called' to join us. So we carried on with one working team, fitting in as many weekends as Reverend Norman and Eirlys Barr were able to manage.

Chapter Thirty-one

Expansion

I don't want to give the impression that our Marriage Encounter Weekends were always serious, or that we never had any problems, or even that every couple who booked on a weekend found it helpful. Although we believed the overwhelming majority of couples benefited greatly from the experience, sometimes a couple would arrive who had not read the information leaflet properly and whose expectations were not met.

Each weekend was a highly disciplined, hardworking forty-four hours, and some had not fully taken this on board. Occasionally, a couple would come with tennis racquets, swimming costumes or walking boots and were disappointed when we told them that their only leisure time would be a short two-hour break on Saturday afternoon!

Then there were the couples who were determined to 'do their own thing'. On one weekend, a couple came with a great deal of luggage but all became clear when, early on the Saturday morning, the husband produced a large karaoke machine, a guitar and several backing tapes, and offered to entertain us all! We managed to persuade him to postpone his performance until Sunday afternoon when we would be saying our farewells to each other over tea and cake. In the event, our final half hour together was spent listening to a pleasant rendering of love songs and romantic ballads, sung directly to his wife. Theirs had been a very good weekend!

On another Friday evening, a black couple arrived – wreathed in smiles – and it was immediately obvious that the wife was heavily pregnant.

After greeting them both and helping the husband to carry their cases to the bedroom, we casually asked when the baby was due. His wife beamed at us.

"Tomorrow!" she replied happily.

As you may guess, the following day the entire team was on red alert, watching for any sign that the newcomer was about to make an appearance. We need not have worried. The couple had a highly successful weekend, and their new baby was born a few days later.

Although we booked venues all around Britain, some couples chose not to attend a weekend close to their home. It was not unusual for a couple to travel from Yorkshire down to Hertfordshire, or a Hampshire couple to book on a weekend in Doncaster. Some made it part of a holiday, touring the surrounding countryside before or after their weekend.

On a weekend held at the Watermill in Berkhamsted, we noticed that one couple spoke with a Scottish accent and discovered that they lived in Arbroath on the north east coast of Scotland. The husband worked on an oil-rig in the North Sea, working two weeks at sea and spending two weeks at home. He had read about Marriage Encounter whilst on the rig and they had made a journey of over 500 miles to be with us.

At the close, the husband was most enthusiastic about all that he and his wife had learned, and asked if we would consider holding a weekend in their area. After some discussion, we promised that if he could guarantee eight couples would attend, we would travel north to his home town.

A few weeks later, he rang to tell us that he had fulfilled his part of the agreement, so the whole team travelled to the historic seaside town of Montrose in Angus, where accommodation had been booked in a three star hotel. However, when we arrived we discovered that all the couples were members of the same Baptist Church and knew each other very well. For once, we were the ones who felt 'shy'! In the event, the weekend was a great success. Not only did we have a great many laughs together, we learned a lot of Scottish dialect words as well!

Not all our weekends were held in hotels. In order to cover some areas of the country, we had to book accommodation in hostels or Diocesan

Centres – and the rooms and food varied considerably depending on who were the main users of the premises.

One of our venues in the early days was predominantly used by church youth groups and outward bound parties, and the meals were usually 'self-catered' – cooked by the groups of youths or hikers who were staying there.

On our arrival, the team was given a bundle of clean sheets and found we were responsible for making-up all the beds. So we hurriedly set to and did this to the best of our ability. However, when it came to meals, we had arranged for the warden and his assistant to provide them for us. We soon discovered that they were not chefs! Throughout the weekend, it was a case of baked potatoes with everything, but the problem was they were not washed thoroughly before they were put into the oven, so they were always 'enhanced' by a layer of grit! The lettuce in the salads was obviously washed with similar care – and was certainly not suitable for vegetarians!

Another venue was a Diocesan Centre in Lancashire, which had been converted from a wealthy mill-owner's mansion. It stood in beautiful grounds and had the most wonderful plaster ceilings and oak-panelled rooms. A modern wing had been built on at the back with a number of single bedrooms down either side of it. These were used during Retreat Weekends.

As *our* weekend was for married couples, single rooms were obviously far from ideal. Our first task on arrival was to move half of the single beds across the corridor to create twin-bedded rooms – and take armchairs and writing desks in the opposite direction to form sitting rooms. Although this involved us in a lot of hard work before the weekend had even begun, the couples had the benefit of two rooms – a sitting room and twin bedroom.

Even so, when they arrived and were given *two* room numbers as they booked in, the look of horror on their faces had to be seen to be believed!

One weekend held at this Centre did not get off to a good start. It was our custom, as team members, to send instructions to couples who had booked on a weekend with details of how to get to the venue. Although occasionally the odd couple would arrive a few minutes late, we allowed for this in our timetable and very rarely did anyone miss the beginning of the first talk.

However, on this particular Friday evening a number of couples arrived at the last minute and one couple – a Baptist minister and his wife from Nottingham – had still not arrived by the time the first talk was due to begin. We telephoned their home number and were told they were 'on their way'. As we were not taking the first session, Anita and I waited anxiously in the entrance hall for their arrival.

They eventually drove up about an hour late and although we made them tea and tried to give them a warm welcome, the husband in particular was cross and impatient with us. Unfortunately our directions on how to reach the Centre were out of date. There had been several recent changes in road numbers and alterations to junctions which had caused them to get lost.

By the following morning, however, we had been forgiven and the couple – Reverend Cliff Dunn and his wife Gail – went on to have a great weekend. By the time it had concluded they were very enthusiastic and saw the work as really valuable. A short time later, after much consideration and prayer, they decided to join the team.

And so, after an unpromising start, we had recruited our second Pastoral couple, enabling us to form two separate Marriage Encounter teams. The work was growing, and Anita and I thought that from now on we would be able to take things a little easier. How wrong we were!

Chapter Thirty-two

Turkey

In the early months of 1990, a couple from Yorkshire with rather unusual occupations booked on a weekend. The husband was employed in translating the bible into Turkish, and they both spent a great deal of time in Turkey – a Muslim country – talking to the locals about Christianity and distributing bibles to anyone who was interested. There was a fair amount of risk involved in this activity, as the Authorities did not view it favourably.

The couple – Rosamund and Graham – found the weekend to be very helpful, and at its close asked to talk with the team. They told us there were a number of European and American couples in Turkey whom they thought might benefit from a Marriage Encounter weekend. As missionaries, they tried to fit in with the customs of the country, and as a result, lived separate lives. Husbands and wives were often separated from each other when they attended social functions (as men and women tended not to intermingle in public) and they frequently ate separately at events arranged by Turkish friends. Consequently, some of their marriages were under strain, and a weekend in which the couples could spend time together and communicate deeply with each other would be just what the doctor ordered!

The Marriage Encounter Team said they were willing to make the journey and Rosamund told us that on her next visit to Turkey in a few weeks' time she would try to recruit couples for the weekend and find accommodation for the team. We left the matter in her hands and as we had elected to pay all expenses ourselves, hoped she would find some suitable – but economic – accommodation.

A few weeks later, Rosamund got in touch to say that a good number of couples had indicated that they would appreciate a Weekend, and that a suitable hotel, with double bedrooms and a conference room, had been located in Yalova, a province of Turkey in the Marmara Region, famous for its thermal baths, apples and forests.

When the team enquired into flights, however, we realised once again (as we had found when travelling to Oberammergau) that charter flights required one to have a week's holiday! Anita and I discovered that, travelling from Manchester, we would have to fly out and return on successive Tuesdays. Other Team Couples, travelling from other destinations, would have to fly on Wednesdays or Thursdays.

However, we all agreed that these variations would not interfere with running our weekend (from Friday to Sunday) so, having heard that Rosamund had managed to arrange simple Bed and Breakfast accommodation for us all in a hotel in the centre of Istanbul for £5.00 per person per night, we booked our flights.

On Tuesday 11th September 1990, our son David drove Anita and me to Manchester Airport and, clutching our hand luggage which, for security, contained all our talks, we boarded the aircraft. It was dark when we arrived at Istanbul's Atatürk International Airport but we were met by Rosamund, who called a taxi and accompanied us to our hotel which was situated in a narrow backstreet in the centre of old Istanbul.

Since our visit, we have spoken to many people who have spent wonderful holidays in luxurious hotels in Turkey, but our hotel was certainly not in that category. We walked into a grubby, dimly-lit foyer containing a few tables and chairs and a reception desk which was manned (so we were told) twenty four hours a day. We did not understand the significance of this until later.

It was almost midnight and by then we were all feeling very tired so we made our way up the stairs, dropped Rosamund off at her door, and continued along the corridor until we reached our room. We discovered that it was extremely small and very dirty. It contained a rickety cupboard and two single beds – one along each wall with a two foot gap between them. The en-suite bathroom contained, in theory, everything that was required, but the toilet bowl was encrusted with lime, stained dark brown and stood three feet from the floor. The shower cascaded from the ceiling directly onto the bathroom floor and immediately beneath it was the only electric power point in the room. Drying ones hair was going to be a hazardous occupation!

When Anita drew back the blankets, she was convinced the beds had already been slept in, but bravely laying the clean white bath towels which we had brought with us over the soiled sheets, we undressed cagily, killed two mosquitoes, cleaned our teeth in a cup of bottled water, got into bed and settled down to sleep as best we could.

As there were a few days before we were due to travel to our 'Marriage Encounter' hotel in Marmara, Rosamund (whose single bedroom we discovered did not even have a window!) acted as our guide in Istanbul and took us to see the sights. We took a bus to explore the Topkapi Palace and Gardens (which were crowded with visitors), and then walked through a network of narrow streets to the Spice Bazaar which seemed to us like an Aladdin's cave. There we drank our first Turkish coffee and ate sticky sweet baklavas.

In the evening, we went to a Kebab House to try authentic Turkish food. We sampled kebabs, and for dessert had three different sweetmeats and a glass of salty drinking yoghurt, which was unusual but surprisingly quenching. As we made our way back to our hotel we felt slightly more acclimatized to our unusual surroundings.

The following day Bill and Brenda Reynolds joined us and by Thursday, our Marriage Encounter team was complete. We spent the day sightseeing, exploring the narrow streets and paying a visit to the famous Blue Mosque, with its wonderful mosaics, six minarets and numerous domes. To celebrate everyone's safe arrival Rosamund suggested we should have a meal together at a local restaurant, so in the evening we set off to one which was highly recommended.

On Rosamund's advice we ordered a meze – a selection of cold and hot food served in small dishes which are placed in the centre of the table.

There were vine leaves stuffed with peppers, meat and tomatoes; puff pastry with cheese and spinach; a spicy dish made from chilli, tomato and chives; and aubergines filled with meat, onion and spices. This was followed by kebabs and lava bread. Anita cautiously avoided having any meat – choosing instead to have vegetables, bread and salad – and her decision to become a temporary vegetarian was a wise one, although I didn't know it at the time. We returned to our seedy hotel in high spirits, looking forward to our journey across the Bosphorus Strait on the following morning, and the Marriage Encounter weekend in Marmara.

During the night, I began to feel extremely nauseous and dizzy and had to get up several times to use our dark brown toilet. By the time morning came, I was unable to stand and felt so ill that it seemed impossible that I would be able to travel that day, much less help to run a Marriage Encounter weekend. Eventually, Anita went down to breakfast alone to break the bad news to the rest of the team.

The next forty-five minutes are difficult to describe. I was alone in the room and lay in my narrow bed, facing the wall and feeling very unwell. I slipped in and out of consciousness, dozing periodically for a minute or two and then awakening again feeling terrible. I wondered how the rest of the team would cope without me – and what Anita and I would do when the others left at lunchtime.

Occasionally I uttered a few words of prayer, expressing my anxiety and groaning now and then as another wave of sickness swept over me. Suddenly I became aware that the wall above me was filled with a strong light, as though someone had switched on a lamp outside the room which was shining in through the window. I felt confused and uneasy, but not afraid, and began to pray quietly under my breath. I seemed to recognise that the 'power' – or whatever it was – was from God and became filled with a strong conviction that "everything is going to be alright".

The light faded, but the conviction became even stronger. I lay still for a few minutes. Then, cautiously, I sat up in bed and realised that I no longer felt nauseous. I assessed my condition and found that all my symptoms seemed to have disappeared. I was just about to get out of bed when Anita came into the room.

"I've explained to everyone that you're ill," she said. "They've suggested that they travel today as arranged, and we should follow on tomorrow if you're better."

"It's OK," I replied, "Everything's going to be alright. I feel much better already!"

I found it difficult to explain exactly what had happened, but as Anita watched me dress, she realised that a remarkable recovery had taken place.

When I went downstairs about twenty minutes later, I was greeted with gasps of surprise and enquiries about my health from Rosamund and the other members of the team. I said that I felt much better and that everything was going to be alright. I didn't mention the word "miracle".

Chapter Thirty–three

A New Chapter

We boarded the catamaran at Istanbul's YeniKapi Feribot Terminali at lunchtime and were soon skidding across the waves to Yalova on the south shore of the Sea of Marmara. From there, we caught a minibus to our hotel and began to prepare for the weekend. Throughout the journey everyone had kept asking after my health and seemed amazed that I had thrown off my sickness so quickly.

The hotel was large but it didn't have a welcoming air about it – although our room *did* contain a double bed, a great improvement on the narrow, single ones in Istanbul. We prepared the conference room and, whilst the others went for a swim in the hot springs nearby, Anita and I went out to buy some bread, bottled water and cheese before resting in our room.

At around seven o'clock the couples began to arrive and soon the weekend was underway. It was not remarkable in any way, as far as we could tell, except for the fact that one of the American wives was very much into cross stitch and carried her bag containing wool, frame and needles with her wherever she went. Throughout the weekend, whenever she sat down – be it at mealtimes or to listen to a talk – she would produce her work bag and stitch away automatically whilst carrying on a conversation or listening attentively to what was being said. It is the only weekend I can remember when every session was accompanied by the clicking of needles and the swish of thread!

We travelled back across the Sea of Marmara to our seedy hotel in Istabul on Monday afternoon and Anita and I decided to have an early night as we had to leave on a dawn flight on the Tuesday morning.

Rosamund kindly insisted on getting up at 3.30 a.m. to see us off in the taxi, although we tried to dissuade her.

It was still dark when the alarm clock rang, but we rose quickly, washed, dressed and packed the final few items into our suitcase before making our way along the landing to where Rosamund was already waiting for us.

We went downstairs together, but as we arrived in the entrance hall Anita and I stopped in amazement. Most of the chairs were occupied by blond-haired young women wearing short skirts and smoking cigarettes. They casually glanced up as we entered but continued with their conversations.

We handed in our key and Rosamund asked the night porter to ring for a taxi. Seeing the surprised looks on our faces, she whispered, "You are right, it's a brothel. I didn't tell you before because I thought you might worry – but you have been perfectly safe here. I know the manager."

All at once a number of puzzling episodes made sense. Although the hotel had appeared to be empty, Anita and I had often heard footsteps in the corridor outside our room during the night. Now we knew the reason for it!

Again, we had been surprised to find there was only one table set for breakfast every morning – the one that was laid for our group. And we had noticed that everything on the table was pre-packed – the plates contained small individual packs of butter, cheese, and jam. The tea (or chai) was served in separate cups and we discovered after a day or two that it was being bought from a shop further down the street and carried back to our dining room by the waiter.

This all made sense now as we realised that the main business of the hotel was certainly not providing bed and breakfast! Rosamund had booked us in there because it was cheap!

Almost before we had time to think about the situation, our taxi drew up at the door and, having said goodbye to Rosamund, we were soon on our way to the airport. A few hours later, back home in Rochdale, we talked over what had been a very different – and remarkable – week's holiday.

* * *

We had now been involved in the Marriage Encounter movement for almost twelve years and during that time our circumstances had gradually changed.

David and Lisa, our children, had grown up and become independent. David had begun to climb the promotional ladder at Rochdale Borough Council and Lisa was spending most of each year working abroad as a Holiday Representative for a major travel company.

For a while, Anita and I had been wondering if it was time for us to withdraw from Marriage Encounter. We were getting older, and felt that perhaps we should be making way for younger people to be on the Team as perhaps their life-style might be more relatable to younger couples than ours was. Also, marriage was becoming less popular and many young people were simply living together. As it was essential that a couple should be married before they booked on a weekend, we were getting fewer bookings than when Baptist Marriage Encounter had begun in 1981.

There was another factor that was influencing us too. Although the weekends were intended to strengthen already sound marriages – "Make your good marriage great!" – we observed that a small percentage of couples were enrolling in a final attempt to revive their failing marriage. Once or twice, we discovered (often by chance) that a couple had been living apart for several weeks, or even months, before booking a weekend! Sometimes their faith paid off and they went away saying they had a 'new marriage', but in other cases their problems were much too fundamental and long-standing to be solved in 44 hours.

Occasionally, a couple would knock on the door of our hotel room to talk with us about a seemingly insoluble problem in their relationship. The causes were diverse: serious sexual dysfunction, an elderly relative's interference, difficulties caused by an errant teenager, and so on. We would listen, helping them to talk to each other about the problem and at times pointing them to an agency which we thought could be of assistance, for we knew the help they required was beyond that which we were qualified to give.

As a result, Anita and I became convinced that we needed training in some form of counselling in order to acquire the skills we needed to help couples in failing marriages. We explored various avenues to training. Eventually I embarked on an Advanced Diploma in Counselling course at Sheffield Hallam Technical College, whilst Anita applied to train with *Relate*, the old Marriage Guidance Council.

In October 1994 Anita and I led the Baptist Marriage Encounter Weekend at Wistaston Hall, near Crewe, knowing that it would be our final one. We had given a year's notice to our fellow team members – who had become dear friends – and the time had now come for us to depart. The weekend went without a hitch, but it was difficult to keep our emotions under control as it drew to a close.

When the last Weekend Couple had driven away, the rest of the team prayed with us, asking God to guide us in whatever the future might bring. Then they presented us with a specially commissioned plate as a memento of the past twelve years with the Movement.

We shed a few tears as we drove away, but felt that it was the right time to move on. We were also sure that the close friendships we had with other team members would continue. Because of the work we had done together, we knew each other so intimately that there was no way we would drift apart – even though hundreds of miles separated our homes.

We were ready to begin a new chapter in our lives. We did not know what the future might bring or where it would find us, but we wondered whether it could possibly contain as many miracles as we had seen since that sunny summer holiday in York.

Epilogue

After we left Marriage Encounter, both Anita and I trained in different aspects of counselling. I attended Sheffield Hallam Technical College (now University) and gained an Advanced Diploma in Counselling, and Anita trained with Relate and worked for a time at the Rochdale Office helping couples who were having difficulties in their marriage.

Eventually we joined forces and did some 'couple counselling' from home. We did not advertise this service but several couples who had heard about us from friends or at church sought us out and booked sessions with us.

We also followed some individual interests. Anita joined the United Christian Singers – a large choir drawn from various churches throughout Manchester – which gave concerts in the city and surrounding areas. I became a member of Touchstones Creative Writing group, which met monthly in the Rochdale Heritage Centre.

We also had our share of ill health. In 2007 Anita had an 'autoimmune' heart attack which was treated successfully and in 2008 she had a stent fitted in an artery adjacent to her heart.

In 2011, I was diagnosed with lung cancer. I was treated at the Christie Hospital with two cycles of chemotherapy and 33 consecutive days of radiotherapy. The cancer was stabilised and, against all the odds, I recovered. During the treatment Anita drove me to the hospital every day – a round trip of 30 miles – and when I was admitted for two weeks she visited daily.

Sadly, on November, 3rd 2017 following a series of seizures in which her immune system attacked her own brain, Anita died peacefully in hospital surrounded by all the members of her family.

And so ends 'The Story of a Marriage' – *our* marriage – and a relationship that lit up my life for fifty-six years. I am so thankful to have been part of it.